ESSENTIAL
QUESTIONS

Other ASCD books by Jay McTighe and Grant Wiggins

Schooling by Design: Mission, Action, and Achievement

Understanding by Design Expanded 2nd edition

The Understanding by Design Guide to Advanced Concepts in Creating and Reviewing Units

The Understanding by Design Guide to Creating High-Quality Units

The Understanding by Design Professional Development Workbook

ESSENTIAL QUESTIONS

Opening Doors to Student Understanding

JAY MCTIGHE ▪ GRANT WIGGINS

Alexandria, Virginia USA

1703 N. Beauregard St. • Alexandria, VA 22311-1714 USA
Phone: 800-933-2723 or 703-578-9600 • Fax: 703-575-5400
Website: www.ascd.org • E-mail: member@ascd.org
Author guidelines: www.ascd.org/write

Gene R. Carter, *Executive Director;* Mary Catherine (MC) Desrosiers, *Chief Program Development Officer;* Richard Papale, *Publisher;* Laura Lawson, *Acquisitions Editor;* Julie Houtz, *Director, Book Editing & Production;* Darcie Russell, *Editor;* Louise Bova, *Senior Graphic Designer;* Mike Kalyan, *Production Manager;* Circle Graphics, Inc., *Typesetter;* Andrea Wilson, *Production Specialist*

ASCD Member Book, No. FY13-6 (April 2013, PSI+). ASCD Member Books mail to Premium (P), Select (S), and Institutional Plus (I+) members on this schedule: Jan., PSI+; Feb., P; Apr., PSI+; May, P; July, PSI+; Aug., P; Sept., PSI+; Nov., PSI+; Dec., P. Select membership was formerly known as Comprehensive membership.

PAPERBACK ISBN: 978-1-4166-1505-7   ASCD product # 109004
Also available as an e-book (see Books in Print for the ISBNs).

Quantity discounts: 10–49 copies, 10%; 50+ copies, 15%; for 1,000 or more copies, call 800-933-2723, ext. 5634, or 703-575-5634. For desk copies: www.ascd.org/deskcopy

Library of Congress Cataloging-in-Publication Data

McTighe, Jay, author.
  Essential questions : opening doors to student understanding / Jay McTighe and Grant Wiggins.
    p. cm.
  Includes bibliographical references and index.
  ISBN 978-1-4166-1505-7 (pbk.)
  1. Questioning. 2. Inquiry-based learning. I. Wiggins, Grant P., 1950- author. II. Title.
  LB1027.44.M38 2013
  371.3'7–dc23
                          2012042589

22 21 20 19 18 17 16 15 14 13 1 2 3 4 5 6 7 8 9 10 11 12

ESSENTIAL QUESTIONS

Opening Doors to Student Understanding

Foreword

We are off and running from the opening page. Plunging right into what matters most, Jay McTighe and Grant Wiggins engage us in an exercise to determine what is *not* an essential question. They ask us to deliberate. We stop, think, and reflect on crafting our questions and consider the impact linguistic choices have on our learners. As readers, we are immediately drawn into vibrant inquiry.

Arguably, questioning is the most timeless and fundamental stratagem employed by teachers from Confucius to Aristotle to Descartes to provoke learners. In the past 20 years, the role of the essential question has risen as a curricular compass, setting the pathway for the learner, due in no small measure to the power of models such as Understanding by Design. The demand for high-quality essential questions is ubiquitous, yet there is a chasm between good intention and the ability to write them well. With the current scrutiny on teacher effectiveness, the emphasis on standards alignment, and the renewed focus on formative assessment, the release of this book is exquisitely timed if not prescient. We need this book now.

Not only is this book a manual that teaches us how to style questions, it is an engaging treatise on transforming instructional inquiry. The authors' pedagogical exploration will directly serve our school-age learners by leading professional educators to revisit and refine practices. They employ fresh language that grabs our attention: "interrogating the content," "tentative closure," and "organizational culture of questioning." It is a riveting read. Deepening the investigation, the authors crystallize the notion that essential question formation is the study of a specialized and potent genre.

In their workshop presentations, Jay and Grant frequently employ sports analogies, and so it is that we are coached actively through these pages. Accessible and eminently useful, *Essential Questions* provides viable rationales for using essential questions, a defining range of essential question types, a design process for shaping them, strategies for effective implementation, and considerations for special situations. We are mentored through a clear eight-phase model to construct questions, deliver them, and consider the responses of our students. The model is supported with myriad examples in clear tables and charts providing a user-friendly touchstone for classroom teachers and professional developers.

For those of us concerned about modernizing learning with digital tools, social media, and global connectivity, a central question is how to support student self-navigation. In this book I found a great revelation in the section on supporting student autonomy. Not only are we given support on how to bring essential questions into our interactions with learners, but we are also given thoughtful assistance on supporting independence for our students. The rubric for building student autonomy is a tremendous contribution to supporting emerging instructional approaches for this century.

Based on years of experience in schools across the United States and the world, Jay and Grant know that is not enough to create an essential question. The culture of each classroom determines whether risks are taken and meaning is made. A compelling discussion in the book is the exploration of how to cultivate a learning environment conducive to mutual respect and connection. We are coached on how to nurture this supportive culture in our classrooms and encouraged to ensure that these same characteristics are mirrored among faculty and school leadership. In a very real sense, Jay and Grant are integrating their work on *Schooling by Design* with their examination of the necessary cultural conditions to enliven essential questioning. They have refreshed and expanded the value of respectful discourse among professionals necessary for an "essential school" as the late Theodore Sizer espoused.

The book is a homage to collaboration. Admired for their models and prolific writing, Jay and Grant represent the power of intellectual kinship and collegial productivity. It has been my pleasure to know these gentlemen for many years, and I can only imagine the e-mail exchanges, the phone calls, the negotiations, the debates, and the serial epiphanies exuded in their compositional process. Yet, what is distinctive is that this book speaks with one voice and offers essential lessons from these teammates who are relentless investigative partners.

In a search for a synonym, I entered the word *essential* into a visual thesaurus application, and the word *marrow* emerged on my computer screen defined as "the choicest or most vital part of some idea or experience." For those educators seeking the choicest curriculum and vitality in learning, what we have in our hands is bound to be a classic cornerstone.

Heidi Hayes Jacobs
Curriculum Designers
The Curriculum 21 Project

What Makes a Question Essential?

Teachers regularly pose questions to their students, but the purpose and form of these questions can vary widely. This book is about a particular kind of question—one we call "essential." So, what makes a question "essential"? Let us begin by engaging you in a bit of inquiry using the following concept-attainment exercise to examine the characteristics of an essential question. The exercise has three parts, as explained in the next several paragraphs.

First, examine the questions in the two columns and try to determine the distinguishing characteristics of the ones labeled "Essential" compared to those labeled "Not Essential." What traits do the essential questions have in common? How do they differ from the others?

Essential Questions

- How do the arts shape, as well as reflect, a culture?
- What do effective problem solvers do when they get stuck?
- How strong is the scientific evidence?
- Is there ever a "just" war?
- How can I sound more like a native speaker?
- Who is a true friend?

Not Essential Questions

- What common artistic symbols were used by the Incas and the Mayans?
- What steps did you follow to get your answer?
- What is a variable in scientific investigations?
- What key event sparked World War I?
- What are common Spanish colloquialisms?
- Who is Maggie's best friend in the story?

Second, look at these additional examples, organized by subject area, to spark your thinking and clarify the qualities of essential questions, or EQs.

Essential Questions in History and Social Studies

- Whose "story" is this?
- How can we know what *really* happened in the past?
- How should governments balance the rights of individuals with the common good?
- Should _____ (e.g., immigration, media expression) be restricted or regulated? When? Who decides?
- Why do people move?
- Why is that there? (geography)
- What is worth fighting for?

Essential Questions in Mathematics

- When and why should we estimate?
- Is there a pattern?
- How does *what* we measure influence *how* we measure? How does *how* we measure influence *what* we measure (or don't measure)?
- What do good problem solvers do, especially when they get stuck?
- How accurate (precise) does this solution need to be?
- What are the limits of this math model and of mathematical modeling in general?

Essential Questions in Language Arts

- What do good readers do, especially when they don't comprehend a text?
- How does *what* I am reading influence *how* I should read it?
- Why am I writing? For whom?
- How do effective writers hook and hold their readers?
- What is the relationship between fiction and truth?
- How are stories from other places and times about me?

Essential Questions in Science

- What makes objects move the way they do?
- How are structure and function related in living things?
- Is aging a disease?
- Why and how do scientific theories change?
- How can we best measure what we cannot directly see?
- How do we decide what to believe about a scientific claim?

Essential Questions in the Arts

- What can artworks tell us about a culture or society?
- What influences creative expression?

- To what extent do artists have a responsibility to their audiences?
- Do audiences have any responsibility to artists?
- What's the difference between a thoughtful and a thoughtless critique?
- If practice makes perfect, what makes perfect practice?

Essential Questions in World Languages

- What should I do in my head when trying to learn a language?
- How can I express myself when I don't know all the words (of a target language)?
- What am I afraid of in hesitating to speak this language? How can I overcome my hesitancy?
- How do native speakers differ, if at all, from fluent foreigners? How can I sound more like a native speaker?
- How much cultural understanding is required to become competent in using a language?
- How can I explore and describe cultures without stereotyping them?

As a result of comparing essential and nonessential questions and studying the additional examples, you should now have an idea of what makes a question "essential." Here are seven defining characteristics. A good essential question

1. Is *open-ended;* that is, it typically will not have a single, final, and correct answer.
2. Is *thought-provoking* and *intellectually engaging,* often sparking discussion and debate.
3. Calls for *higher-order thinking,* such as analysis, inference, evaluation, prediction. It cannot be effectively answered by recall alone.
4. Points toward *important, transferable ideas* within (and sometimes across) disciplines.
5. Raises *additional questions* and sparks further inquiry.
6. Requires *support* and *justification,* not just an answer.
7. *Recurs* over time; that is, the question can and should be revisited again and again.

How does your working definition compare?

Questions that meet all or most of these criteria qualify as essential. These are questions that are not answerable with finality in a single lesson or a brief sentence—and that's the point. Their aim is to stimulate thought, to provoke inquiry, and to spark more questions, including thoughtful student questions, not just pat answers. They are provocative and generative. By tackling such questions, learners are engaged in *uncovering* the depth and richness of a topic that might otherwise be obscured by simply *covering* it.

Now we present the third part of the concept-attainment exercise. Using the characteristics we presented and those that you noted, which of the following questions do you think are essential? Why?

Question	Is it Essential?
1. In what year was the Battle of Hastings fought?	Yes/No
2. How do effective writers hook and hold their readers?	Yes/No
3. Is biology destiny?	Yes/No
4. Onomatopoeia—what's up with that?	Yes/No
5. What are examples of animals adapting to their environment?	Yes/No
6. What are the limits of arithmetic?	Yes/No

Check your answers against the key on page 15. How did you do? Are you getting a better feel for what makes a question essential? Good! Now we'll probe more deeply to uncover the nuances of EQs.

Two Sides of a Coin

Although we have characterized essential questions as being important for stimulating student thinking and inquiry, this is not their sole function. In the body of work known as Understanding by Design (McTighe & Wiggins, 2004; Wiggins & McTighe, 2005, 2007, 2011, 2012), we propose that education should strive to develop and deepen students' understanding of important ideas and processes so that they can transfer their learning within and outside school. Accordingly, we recommend that content (related goals) be unpacked to identify long-term transfer goals and desired understandings. Part of this unpacking involves the development of associated essential questions. In other words, EQs can be used to effectively frame our key learning goals. For example, if a content standard calls for students to learn about the three branches of government, then questions such as "When does a government overstep its authority?" or "How might we guard against governmental abuses of power?" help stimulate student thinking about why we need checks and balances, what the framers of the Constitution were trying to achieve, and other governmental approaches to balancing power. Note that the question has more than one answer, even if in the United States we have grown accustomed to our particular answer. In this sense, the question is still open, not closed.

We'll have more to say about how to come up with good essential questions in later chapters, but for now try this simple thought experiment. If the content you are expected to teach represents "answers," then what questions were being asked by the people who came up with those answers? This conceptual move offers a useful strategy both for seeing a link between content standards and important questions and for coming up with ways of engaging students in the very kind of thinking that is required to truly understand the content. In short, expert knowledge is the result of inquiry, argument, and difference of opinion; the best questions point to hard-won big ideas that we want learners to come to understand. The questions thus serve as doorways or lenses through which learners can better see and explore the key concepts, themes, theories, issues, and problems that reside within the content.

It is also through the process of actively "interrogating" the content using provocative questions that students strengthen and deepen their understanding. For instance, a regular consideration of the question "How are stories from different places and times about me?" can lead students to the big ideas that great literature explores—the universal themes of the human condition underneath the more obvious peculiarities of personality or culture—and thus can help us gain insight into our own experiences. Similarly, the question "To what extent can people accurately predict the future?" serves as a launch pad for examining big ideas in statistics and science, such as sampling variables, predictive validity, degrees of confidence, and correlation versus causality.

At a practical level, think of targeted understandings and essential questions as the flip sides of the same coin. Our essential questions point toward important transferable ideas that are worth understanding, even as they provide a means for exploring those ideas. This associated relationship is suggested graphically in the Understanding by Design (UbD) unit-planning template, where targeted understandings are placed next to their companion essential questions. Here are some examples:

Understandings	**Essential Questions**
• The geography, climate, and natural resources of a region influence the economy and lifestyle of the people living there.	• How does *where* you live influence *how* you live?
• Statistical analysis and data display often reveal patterns. Patterns enable prediction.	• What will happen next? How sure are you?
• People have different dietary needs based on age, activity level, weight, and various health considerations.	• How can a diet that is "healthy" for one person be unhealthy for another?
• Dance is a language of shape, space, timing, and energy that can communicate ideas and feelings.	• How can motion express emotion?

Three Connotations of *Essential*

A finer-grained examination of such questions reveals three different but overlapping meanings for the term *essential*. One meaning of *essential* includes the terms "important" and "timeless." Essential questions in this sense arise naturally and recur throughout one's life. Such questions are broad in scope and universal by nature. *What is justice? Is art a matter of taste or principles? How much should we tamper with our own biology and chemistry? Is science compatible with religion? Is an author's view privileged in determining the meaning of a text?* Essential questions of this type are common and perpetually arguable. We may arrive at or be helped to grasp understandings for these questions, but we soon learn that answers to them are provisional or more varied than we might have imagined. In other words, we are liable to change our minds in response to reflection, different views, and rich experience concerning such questions as we go through life—and such changes of mind are not only expected but beneficial. A good education is grounded in such lifelong questions, even if we sometimes lose sight of them while focusing on content mastery. Such questions signal that education is not just about learning "the answer" but also about learning how to think, question, and continually learn.

A second connotation for *essential* refers to "elemental" or "foundational." Essential questions in this sense reflect the key inquiries within a discipline. Such questions point to the big ideas of a subject and to the frontiers of technical knowledge. They are historically important and very much alive in the field. The question "Is any history capable of escaping the social and personal history of its writers?" has been widely and heatedly debated among scholars over the past hundred years, and it compels novices and experts alike to ponder potential bias in any historical narrative. Questions such as "How many dimensions are there in space-time?" and "To what extent are current global weather patterns typical or unusual?" are at the forefront of debate about string theory in physics and global climate change in climatology, respectively. The question "Is it more a sign of creativity or arrogance when a writer tries to tell a story from the perspective of a gender or culture different from his or her own?" has been energetically debated in the world of literature and the arts in recent years.

A third and important connotation for the term *essential* refers to what is vital or necessary for personal understanding—in the case of schooling, what students need for learning core content. In this sense, a question can be considered essential when it helps students make sense of seemingly isolated facts and skills or important but abstract ideas and strategies—findings that may be understood by experts but not yet grasped or seen as valuable by the learner. Examples include questions such as these: *In what ways does light act wavelike? How do the best writers hook and hold their readers? What models best describe a business cycle? What is the "best fit" line of these "messy" data points?* By actively exploring such questions, learners are helped to connect disparate and confusing information and arrive at important understandings as well as more effective (transfer) applications of their knowledge and skill. Consider a sports example. In soccer, basketball, football, lacrosse, and water polo, strategic players and teams come to understand the importance of asking "Where can we best create more open space on offense?" (Note that this question serves as a springboard for a strategic understanding—that spreading out the defense enhances ball advancement and scoring opportunities.) It leads to the more obvious and important question: "How might we win more games?" Note, therefore, that even in skill-focused instruction such as in PE or math, there are important essential questions for helping students understand the point of the skills and the meaning of results. (We will further discuss EQs in skill-based courses in later chapters.)

Intent Trumps Form

You may have heard that so-called higher-order questions should begin with the stems *why, how,* or *in what ways.* Indeed, such question starters seem to signal inherently open-ended thought, inviting multiple responses. Do not assume, however, that all questions beginning with *what, who,* or *when* are necessarily asking for factual answers or that *why* questions are inherently higher-order. For example, consider these questions: *What is fair in economics? Who is a "winner"? When should we fight?* These are clearly not recall questions. They encourage thinking and discussion, and one's answers may evolve over time. Alternately, you could ask your class, "Why did World War II start?" but really be seeking the single answer that is provided in the textbook.

This consideration leads to a more general point: intent trumps form. *Why* you ask a question (in terms of the desired result of asking it) matters more than *how* you phrase it. No question is inherently essential or trivial. Whether it is essential depends on purpose, audience, context, and impact. What do you as a teacher intend for students to do with the question? Recall the earlier example "Is biology destiny?" It is framed in a way that to the uninitiated might sound closed or factual. But clearly we would ask it to spark interesting and pointed debate about what is and isn't predictable about human behavior and health. In other words, the essentialness of the question depends upon why we pose it, how we intend students to tackle it, and what we expect for the associated learning activities and assessments. Do we envision an open, in-depth exploration, including debate, of complex issues, or do we plan to simply lead the students to a prescribed answer? Do we hope that our questions will spark students to raise their own questions about a text, or do we expect a conventional interpretation?

In other words, if we look only at the wording of a question out of context, we cannot tell whether the question is or is not essential. Consider the question "What is a story?" Clearly, if we pose this question with the intent of having students give a textbook answer ("a story contains a plot, characters, setting, and action"), then the question (as pursued) is not essential in terms of our criteria. However, if the question is being asked to initially elicit well-known story elements but then *overturn* that conventional definition through a study of postmodern novels that lack one or more of these elements, then it functions in an "essential" manner.

Consider the same question—"What's the pattern?"—used in three classroom situations with very different intentions:

1. A 2nd grade teacher asks, "Boys and girls, look at the numbers 2, 4, 6, 8, ___. What comes next? What's the pattern?" In this case, the question is leading toward a specific answer (10).

2. An Algebra 1 teacher presents students with a set of data and asks them to plot two related variables on a graph. "What do you notice? What's the pattern?" In this case, the teacher is guiding the students to see a linear relationship in all the data.

3. A science teacher shows a data table of incidents of AIDS cases over a 15-year period, disaggregated by age, gender, region, and socioeconomic status. His question to students is "What's the pattern (or patterns)?" Instead of a pat answer, he intends to evoke careful analysis, reasoning, and spirited discussion.

Thus we cannot say a question is or is not essential based only on the language used in its phrasing. As noted, *who/what/when* questions, as well as those that seem to elicit a *yes/no* response, may spark impressive curiosity, thought, and reflection in students, depending upon how they are set up instructionally and the nature of the follow-ups. Consider these examples and imagine the lively discussion, sustained thinking, and insights they might evoke:

- Is the universe expanding?
- Is a democracy that suspends freedoms a contradiction in terms?
- Does Euclidean geometry offer the best "map" for the space we live in?
- Who should lead?
- Are imaginary numbers useful?
- Is *Catcher in the Rye* a comedy or a tragedy?
- What is the "third" world? Is there a "fourth"?
- When is mission accomplished and victory assured?

And as we noted, the notion of intent works the other way around. A teacher may pose an intriguing and *seemingly* open question yet expect a pat answer. In the worst cases, instructors display intellectual dishonesty when they ask for students' opinions on controversial issues but actually seek or highlight responses that they deem politically or morally correct.

This relevance of purpose or intent is more easily grasped if you think about your own response to thought-provoking questions. The best essential questions are really alive. People ask, discuss, and debate them outside school. They arise naturally in discussion, and they open up thinking and possibilities—for novices and experts alike. They signal that inquisitiveness and open-mindedness are fundamental habits of mind and characteristic of lifelong learners. In a more practical sense, a question is alive in a subject if we really engage with it, if it seems genuine and relevant to us, and if it helps us gain a more systematic and deep understanding of what we are learning.

Ultimately, then, we need to consider the larger intent and context of the question—including its associated follow-ups, assignments, and assessments—to determine whether it ends up being essential. (We have more to say on the culture of inquiry needed to make the most of essential questions in a later chapter.)

Size and Scope Matter: Overarching Versus Topical EQs

Questions such as "What margins of error are tolerable?" are essential in yet another sense. They offer relevance and transferability across disciplines, linking not only to units and courses in measurement, statistics, and engineering, but also to areas as diverse as pottery, music, and parachute packing. Such questions encourage and even demand transfer beyond the particular topic in which we first encounter them. They can (and thus should) recur over the years to promote conceptual connections and curriculum coherence within (and sometimes) across topics and disciplines.

Essential questions (and companion understandings) differ in scope. For example, "What lessons can we learn from World War II?" and "How do the best mystery writers hook and hold their readers?" are typically asked to help students come to particular understandings around those specific topics and skills. Such questions are not usually meant to be perpetually open or unanswerable. They refer specifically to the topic of a unit, in these cases, World War II and the genre of writing called mysteries, respectively. Other essential questions are broad and overarching, taking us beyond any particular topic or skill, toward more general, transferable understandings. For example, "What lessons can we and can't we learn from the past?" extends well beyond World War II and can fruitfully be asked again and again over many years in several subject areas. Similarly, we need not inquire solely about how mysteries engage us. That topical question fits under the broader question that applies to all writers and artists: "How do the best writers and artists capture and hold our attention?"

We refer to specific essential questions as "topical" and the more general questions as "overarching." (The same idea applies to understandings.) Here are some paired examples of these two types of essential questions:

Overarching Essential Questions

- Whose "story" (perspective) is this?
- How are structure and function related?
- In what ways does art reflect, as well as shape, culture?
- How do authors use story elements to establish mood?
- What makes a system?

- What are common factors in the rise and fall of powerful nations?

Topical Essential Questions

- How did Native Alaskans view the "settlement" of their land?
- How does the structure of various insects help them to survive?
- What do ceremonial masks reveal about the Inca culture?
- How does John Updike use setting to establish a mood?
- How do our various body systems interact?
- Why did the Soviet Union collapse?

As you can see, the essential questions on the right focus on particular topics, whereas the companion questions to the left are broader in nature. (Although seemingly convergent, these topical questions still give rise to different plausible responses.) Notice that the overarching EQs make no mention of the *specific* content of the unit. They transcend particular subject matter to point toward broader, transferable understandings that cut across unit (and even course) topics.

Overarching essential questions (and understandings) are valuable for framing entire courses and programs of study (such as a K–12 health curriculum). They provide the conceptual armature for an understanding-based curriculum that spirals around the same EQs across the grades.

Metacognitive and Reflective Questions

The examples of essential questions that we have provided thus far have been primarily nested in academic disciplines. However, there is a more general set of EQs that may be described as metacognitive and reflective. Here are some examples:

- What do I know and what do I need to know?
- Where should I start? When should I change course? How will I know when I am done?
- What's working? What's not? What adjustments should I make?
- Is there a more efficient way to do this? Is there a more effective way to do this? How should I balance efficiency and effectiveness?
- How will I know when I am done?
- What should I do when I get stuck?
- How can I overcome my fear of making mistakes?
- What have I learned? What insights have I gained?
- How can I improve my performance?
- What will I do differently next time?

General questions of this type are truly essential to effective learning and performance, within and outside school. Such questions have proven particularly fruitful in subjects that focus on skill development and performance. Their use characterizes a thoughtful and reflective individual, and they can be posed and considered across the grades, as well as at home and throughout life.

Nonessential Questions

Various types of questions are used in schools, and most are not essential in our sense of the term (even if they all play useful roles in teaching). Let's look at three other types of common classroom questions: questions that lead, guide, and hook. In later chapters we will describe other types, including probing questions and questions used to check for understanding.

Questions That Lead

The legendary comedian Groucho Marx hosted a television quiz show in the 1960s called *You Bet Your Life.* Whenever a contestant missed all or most of the quiz queries, Groucho would pose the final face-saving question: "Who is buried in Grant's tomb?" (Alas, not all contestants could answer it!) This is a perfect example of a leading question because it points to and demands the single, "correct" answer. (We realize that lawyers and debaters define leading questions differently, but we think the term is apt for describing the teacher's motive: to elicit a correct answer.) Here are other examples of leading questions:

- What is seven times six?
- What did we say was true of all four-sided shapes?
- Who was the president at the start of the Great Depression?
- What is the chemical symbol for mercury?
- What's the relative minor key of A major?
- Which letters are vowels?

Leading questions allow a teacher to check that learners can recollect or locate specific information. Thus they have their place when recall and reinforcement of factual knowledge are desired. Another term for such questions is *rhetorical,* which usefully reminds us that they aren't real questions in an important sense. Their purpose is not to signal inquiry but to point to a fact. That's why lawyers and debaters routinely use rhetorical questions to direct attention to *their* point.

Questions That Guide

Another familiar type of question used by teachers (and found in textbooks) may be called "guiding." Consider the following examples:

- Is this sentence punctuated properly?
- Why must the answer be less than zero?
- How do we use the "rule of thirds" in photography?
- Can you state Newton's 2nd Law in your own words?
- When did the main character begin to suspect his former friend?
- What were the four causes of World War I? (This information is found on different pages in the text.)
- Which words tend to be feminine and which masculine in French?

Questions that guide are broader than questions that lead, but are not truly open-ended or designed to cause in-depth inquiry. Each of these questions is steering the student toward previously targeted knowledge and skill—to arrive at a definite answer. Yet the answer requires some inference, not simply recall. As such they are important tools for helping teachers achieve specific content outcomes.

Although such questions are familiar and useful, we do not consider them essential, as you will see if you check them against the seven criteria noted earlier. They may be fruitfully employed during one or more lessons, but they are not intended to set up a long-term inquiry and will not be revisited over an extended time period.

Questions That Hook

The best teachers have long recognized the value of hooking students' attention at the start of a new lesson, unit, or course. Indeed, clever opening questions can spark interest, capture imagination, and set up wonder. Although we most certainly encourage the use of questions that hook students' interest, they differ from essential questions. Consider two examples of "hooks" to see how they are distinguished from associated essential questions:

1. To open a unit on nutrition for 6th graders, a teacher poses the following question: "Can what you eat and drink help prevent zits?" This hook effectively captures students' interest and launches an exploration of the unit's broader EQ: "What should we eat?"

2. A science teacher in an Alaskan village uses this question to hook his students: "Are we drinking the same water as our ancestors?" Given the cultural reverence for ancestors and the significance of the ocean for survival, this is an elegant opener in the context of his school community. It is coupled with the companion essential question "Where does water come from and where does it go?" to spark ongoing inquiry into the relevant science.

Figure 1.1 provides examples that will help you to distinguish among the four types of classroom questions discussed in this chapter, and Figure 1.2 highlights the characteristics of each type.

Figure 1.1 Examples of Four Types of Classroom Questions

Content or Topic	Questions That Hook	Questions That Lead	Questions That Guide	Essential Questions
Nutrition	Can what you eat help prevent zits?	What types of foods are in the food groups?	What is a balanced diet?	What should we eat?
Novel Study on *Catcher in the Rye*	Do you know any teenagers that act crazy? Why do they act that way?	When (time period) and where (location) does the novel take place?	Is Holden normal? (Note: The main character is telling the story from a psychiatric hospital.)	What makes a story timeless? What "truths" can we learn from fiction?
Musical Scales	Do your parents like your music?	What are the notes of the C major scale?	Why would a composer use a major as opposed to a minor scale?	What distinguishes music from "noise"? What influences musical tastes (e.g., culture, age)?
Constitution/Bill of Rights	Do you agree with the "stand your ground" laws?	What is the Second Amendment?	Does the Second Amendment support "stand your ground" laws, according to the courts?	Which constitutional principles are timeless and which should be amended if outdated or outmoded (e.g., only white males were once seen as "persons")? Where is the balance between personal freedoms and the common good? Is the Fourth Amendment or any other parts of the Bill of Rights out of date?
Psychology/Human Behavior	Why do kids sometimes act stupid when they are in groups?	Who was B. F. Skinner? What is behaviorism?	What are the similarities and differences among behaviorism, Gestalt psychology, and Freudian psychology?	Why do people behave as they do?

Figure 1.2 Characteristics of Four Types of Classroom Questions

Questions That Hook
<ul><li>Asked to interest learners around a new topic</li><li>May spark curiosity, questions, or debate</li><li>Often framed in engaging "kid language"</li><li>Asked once or twice, but not revisited</li></ul>

Questions That Lead
<ul><li>Asked to be answered</li><li>Have a "correct" answer</li><li>Support recall and information finding</li><li>Asked once (or until *the* answer is given)</li><li>Require no (or minimal) support</li></ul>

Questions That Guide
<ul><li>Asked to encourage and guide exploration of a topic</li><li>Point toward desired knowledge and skill (but not necessarily to a single answer)</li><li>May be asked over time (e.g., throughout a unit)</li><li>Generally require some explanation and support</li></ul>

Essential Questions
<ul><li>Asked to stimulate ongoing thinking and inquiry</li><li>Raise more questions</li><li>Spark discussion and debate</li><li>Asked and reasked throughout the unit (and maybe the year)</li><li>Demand justification and support</li><li>"Answers" may change as understanding deepens</li></ul>

Summing Up

Classroom questions can be classified into different types, each with different, legitimate purposes. As you consider the appropriate types of questions to include in your teaching, we caution you, however, to distinguish between two connotations of the term *essential:* (1) essential to me in my role as a teacher, where questions that "hook" and "guide" are regularly employed, versus (2) essential for students to continuously examine so as to "come to an understanding" of key ideas and processes. We are using the second meaning in this book. Indeed, in an understanding-focused curriculum, we want more of the latter kinds of questions.

Now that you have a better understanding of what makes a question essential, we will look more closely at when and why we should pose them. (Note: Although you might "get" the idea of essential questions, it doesn't follow that you will necessarily be able to automatically develop great essential questions on your own. We will explore ideas for generating and refining EQs in Chapter 3.)

FAQs

My principal says that we should have at least one essential question for every lesson we teach. I am finding this very hard. Can you help?

In Understanding by Design, we have chosen the unit as a focus for design because the key elements of UbD—transfer goals, understandings, essential questions, and performances of understanding—are too complex and multifaceted to be satisfactorily addressed within a single lesson. In particular, essential questions are meant to focus on long-term learning and thus be revisited over time, not answered by the end of a class period. Not only would it be difficult to come up with a new EQ for every lesson; the predictable result would be a set of superficial (leading) or, at best, guiding questions.

Your principal is presumably well intended, but we would want her to distinguish between *using* EQs on a regular basis (we endorse that) and using a *new* one for each lesson. One or two truly essential questions can be used to frame the learning over the course of many lessons. Perhaps you should give your principal this book!

Answers and Commentary for Exercise on p. 4		
Question	**Is the question essential?**	**Commentary**
1. In what year was the Battle of Hastings fought?	No	This is a factual question with a single correct answer.
2. How do effective writers hook and hold their readers?	Yes	This is a rich question for exploring the many facets of effective writing, including different genres, audience/purpose connections, writer's voice, and organizational structures.
3. Is biology destiny?	Yes	This is intended to be a thought-provoking, open question with many nuances (so don't be fooled by the phrasing).
4. Onomatopoeia—what's up with that?	No	Although the format of the question may wake up a sleepy student, it doesn't really open up worthy inquiry. At best, it can lead to a definition of a new term.
5. What are examples of animals adapting to their environment?	No	This is a useful question for helping students understand the concept of adaptation in various manifestations; however, there are specific answers that could be found in a book.
6. What are the limits of arithmetic?	Yes	This is an open question, widely applicable across mathematical topics across the grades; the question helps students come to understand an abstract yet important idea: mathematics involves tools and methods that have both strengths and limitations.

I'm confused about the difference between guiding and essential questions. Some of the questions you cited as essential—such as "What do the best writers do to hook and hold their readers' attention?"—seem to fit the definition of "guiding" questions: "Not open-ended or designed to cause in-depth inquiry. They are designed to focus learning of content or activities."

You're correct; the difference is a bit subtle. But it all goes back to intent, as we said in this chapter. If the aim is to arrive at a single, final, and not-to-be-questioned answer, then the point of the question is to guide learning toward that answer. But if the point is to *keep questioning,* even if we arrive at a provisional answer that makes sense, then the question is essential.

2

Why Use Essential Questions?

In Understanding by Design and other curriculum planning frameworks, essential questions are often included as an expected element. Why would such questions be required as opposed to optional? In what ways is an educational plan better if it is framed by questions? The short answer is that essential questions make our unit plans more likely to yield focused and thoughtful learning and learners. The best EQs, handled well, make crystal-clear to students that passive learning is a no-no in the classroom; that thinking is required, not optional.

But there are other great reasons for building units around important queries, too. Essential questions:

- Signal that inquiry is a key goal of education.
- Make it more likely that the unit will be intellectually engaging.
- Help to clarify and prioritize standards for teachers.
- Provide transparency for students.
- Encourage and model metacognition for students.
- Provide opportunities for intra- and interdisciplinary connections.
- Support meaningful differentiation.

Let's explore each of these purposes in more detail.

Signaling That Inquiry Is a Key Goal

Successful inquiry leads us to "see" and "grasp" and "make sense" of things that were initially puzzling, murky, or fragmented; thus questioning is meant to culminate in new and more revealing meaning. However, these new meanings are rarely final. Indeed, our goal is for students to become active, probing, and determined inquirers, continually considering important questions and possible meanings. As the child in "The Emperor's New Clothes," Pooh in *Winnie the Pooh,* and

Socrates in Plato's *Dialogues* remind us, to persist in asking the questions when others don't is the key to escaping the bounds of unthinking habit, belief, and dogma. Once we have learned to question—really question—then we are immunized from falling victim to people who want us *not* to think too hard about what they say, be it politicians, advertisers, or bullying associates.

In short, a key long-term goal of education is for students to become better questioners because in the end—with much knowledge made quickly obsolete in the modern world—the ability to question is central to meaningful learning and intellectual achievement at high levels. So, then, what questions would you like students to keep asking even as others may stop asking questions or avoid them altogether? What questions should we persist in addressing, even as we may tire of the challenge of making sense of complex issues and problems? Those are essential questions worth building learning around, regardless of the subject.

As obvious as this may be to readers, our collective actions as educators often suggest a blind spot or contradiction. Study after study has shown that the majority of teachers' questions are leading and low-level, focused on factual knowledge. Here is a brief summary of such findings (Pagliaro, 2011, p. 13):

> Ever since the first reported study on questioning was conducted in 1912, it has been noted that a vast majority of questions asked by teachers are low level (Wragg, 1993; Wilen, 2001; Wragg & Brown, 2001). Moreover, these low-level questions are predominantly asked from the elementary school through university levels (Albergaria-Almeida, 2010). . . . One recent study indicated that teachers ask as many as 300 to 400 questions a day (Levin & Long, 1981). They also tend to ask them in rapid-fire fashion. Teachers in third grade reading groups asked a question every 43 seconds (Gambrel, 1983) and teachers in junior high English classes averaged as many as five questions a minute.

In our many classroom walk-throughs, we have rarely heard *sustained* inquiry into a few compelling questions—even when there is an essential question posted on the whiteboard! Indeed, a great challenge in education—where standards tend to focus on content to be learned rather than inquiries to be sustained—is to avoid a passivity-inducing march through unprioritized content.

In the UbD unit-planning template, essential questions are placed in Stage 1, the location for all unit goals. This placement is meant to signal that the *questions* are an aim, not merely a setup for the answers we want students to learn. The deeper message in calling a question a goal is that developing and deepening understanding, not mere acquisition of content, is a long-term aim of education, and understanding can be furthered only through constant questioning. It is rarely the case that we come to understand a new and complex teaching or experience on first blush. That's why it is proper to say that meaning is made and understanding is earned *over time.* Such outcomes cannot simply be transmitted like factual information or merely practiced like discrete skills. (For more on the distinctions between the goals of meaning and acquisition, see Wiggins & McTighe, 2011, 2012.) Accordingly, essential questions serve as doorways to understanding; that is, by exploring questions, learners are engaged in constructing meaning for themselves.

Making a Unit Intellectually Engaging

A time-honored way to make learning more lively and proactive is to frame school-work around enchanting and thought-provoking questions and to weave the content in as "answers" or "tools" in helping learners address those questions. The best essential questions are thought-provoking by design; that is, by their very nature they seek to bring minds to life. As noted in Chapter 1, a question isn't essential unless it awakens, heightens, or challenges thought.

From a pedagogical point of view, we seek questions that are likely to make students want to do two things: (1) actively pursue an inquiry and not be satisfied with glib, superficial answers, and (2) willingly learn content along the way in the service of the inquiry. That's why the best questions, used properly, make learning more active and enjoyable. When such questions are employed effectively, students experience far less sense of pointless drudgery because they are acquiring knowledge and skill for more obvious and worthy reasons. The learning is thus more intrinsically than extrinsically motivated, making it far more likely that students will persist with the work required for understanding and continuous improvement.

No wonder, then, that simulations, video games, and sports are so engaging and athletes are willing to endure the tedium of skill development and the pain of conditioning. Lurking behind every soccer game or swim meet is a set of interesting and ongoing essential questions: *What do we need to do to win? What do we need to do to improve? What are our strengths and weaknesses, and how can we play to our strengths and lessen our weaknesses?* Such questions are constantly alive because each new game or meet brings a new form of challenge, and using one's mind to figure out how to be better at an immersive challenge is key to motivation.

In fact, the best coaches make such implicit questions explicit. Grant saw this with one of his daughter's high school soccer coaches, a veteran of 40 years of college and high school coaching. Unlike so many of his colleagues, he didn't lecture during the half-time break. He merely asked questions: *What is working for us so far? What isn't? Why isn't it working, and how can we improve it? What is working for the other team, and how can we counter it?* The girls became much better players under this coach even though he "taught" less. As a result of his Socratic methods, they learned to "think soccer" and be constantly intrigued by and alert to the challenges in the questions.

We saw the same effect of good questions used by an English/language arts teacher of 6th grade students. This teacher employed the following essential questions to guide students' writing and the peer reviews:

For writers: *What is your purpose? Who is your audience? Where is the paper working and not working, given your purpose?* The answers had to be stapled to the draft for peer review.

For reviewers: *To what extent did the writer achieve his/her purpose? Where were you most interested and where did you lose interest and why?*

Invariably—as noted by the teacher and by interviewed students—the places where the reader lost interest became a teachable moment for some aspect of idea development, organization, word choice, or mechanics. Thus the framework of the EQs, and the effects of actively asking them, made the learning of the typical content far more relevant, timely, and acceptable to the learners. (Not incidentally, this teacher's students significantly outperformed other students in the district on the state writing assessment.)

Helping to Clarify and Prioritize Standards for Teachers

Nearly every teacher we know faces a common challenge: there is simply too much content and not enough time to teach it all optimally. Yet there is a paradoxical quality to planning and teaching once all the content has been specified: it seems to the teacher as if *everything* is important, and that it is *all* connected—that's why it was chosen! But if everything is important and connected, then *nothing* is self-evidently important *from the learner's perspective.*

You'll recall that one of our criteria for an essential question is that it points to the larger, transferable ideas and processes in standards. Indeed, essential questions offer a practical vehicle for prioritizing the content in the standards and enabling teachers to focus subject matter in a way that makes the key ideas more overt. As teachers have repeatedly told us, working with essential questions helps them to stay focused, separate the intellectual wheat from the chaff, and keep the most important ends—understanding and transfer—in mind. (In the next chapter we provide specific techniques for using essential questions to "unpack" and prioritize standards.)

In subjects like history and science, the need is particularly pressing. Textbooks present endless amounts of information with few organizing structures and, too often, with no obvious relevance or points of intellectual connection for students. When teachers feel compelled to "cover" all the designated content in standards, the result can be a mind-numbing march through unprioritized material with no clear goals or ideas for making sense of the work.

What to do? Here's an example from a global studies teacher who organized his entire course around a set of essential questions.

A set of recurring questions are used to drive the course and permit us to link the content to our lives:

1. How do we identify ourselves?
2. Whom should we care for?
3. What causes conflict? Why do people abuse their power over others?
4. Does global interdependence help or harm the people involved? How do our economic and political choices affect others?
5. Do human beings have rights? Are people "equal"? What does it mean to say that all people have "rights" and are "equal"?
6. What responsibilities do we have to others in the world? What responsibilities do governments have to people? What responsibilities do corporations have to people?
7. Is there right and wrong? If there is right and wrong, how do we come to know it? How does one live in the world with integrity? How well does someone's choices, words, and actions reflect his values?
8. What habits and attitudes do we need to be successful in life? How can this global studies course help?
9. What information should we trust? How do we know what to believe?
10. How do we know what we know about the past? What are the key challenges and responsibilities of historians?

At the beginning of the year, this teacher modeled how to analyze the content using these questions, and he facilitated group discussions. But by spring he had turned the classroom over to the students, whereby it was *their* job to link the most recent lessons (Cuban missile crisis, apartheid, the Arab Spring) to the essential questions on their own. Using a "jigsaw" process, small groups took responsibility for researching a given topic, making connections to designated EQs, and presenting their findings to the class. This set of recurring essential questions brought coherence and relevance to the course while enabling the students to become more effective and autonomous in making rich conceptual connections with the content.

Such prioritization of standards via questions has an added benefit when we run into difficulties with pacing. By building our teaching around a few key questions, and by reinforcing those questions through repeated reference with varying content, we will have far less difficulty giving up bits of content here and there when sickness, snow days, and other inevitable interruptions mess up our planned schedule. Few teachers ever see their best-laid curriculum plans come to fruition flawlessly; no school year is without roadblocks, speed bumps, diversions, or bad luck. But by framing one's work around priority questions, we make it far more likely that learning remains focused, coherent, and less stressful when the unexpected happens.

Providing Transparency for Students

Students arguably face an even more daunting task than teachers. As complete novices, they must not only make sense of each new topic, lesson, and activity, but also figure out what matters most in the confusing buzz of all the new stimuli. In parallel to the focusing role EQs play for teachers, essential questions provide a beacon or touchstone for learners as they continually try to orient themselves in the new world of information they are entering. If students can have faith that a few questions frame all the content and provide an organizing structure for learning, then their anxiety over trying to figure out where the coursework is headed is greatly lessened and their ability to make connections on their own is increased.

Grant repeatedly saw the power of a question to focus learning and lessen student anxiety in his own high school teaching years ago. By posing the essential questions at the start of new units, and by announcing that the questions would be part of the final essay assessment, students were visibly relieved in addition to being more productive. Here are examples from his English teaching:

> **Readings:** "The Emperor's New Clothes," *Oedipus the King,* Plato's "Allegory of the Cave," and "Winnie the Pooh and Piglet Hunt Woozles" from *Winnie the Pooh.*
>
> **Essential Question:** *Who sees and who is blind?*
>
> **Writing:** Journal entries and essays on the essential questions
>
> **Essential Questions:** *What am I trying to say? Have I said it clearly and convincingly? Have I said it in the most engaging way?*

Note that the readings were deliberately chosen to shed light on the question and to provide shifting perspective on possible answers. Moreover, the unit was completely transparent; that is, the students knew that the essential question (*Who sees and who is blind?*) would be the basis for the final essay question, so that their reading, note taking, and discussions were focused from the start.

In the case of the essay writing, further transparency was supported by having the students examine strong and weak examples of nonfiction writing and by having them derive additional criteria by which their own work could be self-assessed, peer reviewed, and judged. (This was years before rubrics were widely used.)

Some teachers have objected that providing such transparency is actually a disservice to students because it co-opts their ability to develop understanding on their own. We think this view is a bit disingenuous. Most experienced and effective teachers know exactly where the unit and course are headed and shape the work accordingly. Why shouldn't the students also know where the course is going, if the aim is productive learning? To see the importance of transparency more clearly, imagine if your supervisors didn't tell you the basis for their evaluations as they observe your teaching and evaluate your performance. Yet this is precisely the student's situation in classrooms where learning and assessment priorities (and evaluative criteria) are vague or mysterious. Our claim here is straightforward: the right questions, made transparent from the start of a course or unit, help rather than hinder students' ability to make meaning, learn effectively, and create worthy products and performances based on their inquiries.

Encouraging and Modeling Metacognition

Essential questions do more than focus the learning for students and teachers. They specifically model the kinds of thinking that students need to emulate and internalize if they are to learn to high levels independently. Put simply, the essential questions model for students the kind of questioning they need to be able to do on their own.

This is one reason why we think it unwise for the students to come up with all the questions to be studied. It is the expert, after all, who knows the most fruitful questions for advancing learning and thinking. Although students can (and are certainly encouraged to) raise and pursue their own questions, the best essential questions reflect expert queries and insights about disciplined inquiry. (We further consider the student's role as instigator of questions and inquiry in Chapter 4.)

This reality is made quite clear in a famous set of essential questions in mathematics around which George Polya (1957) framed his seminal work on problem solving decades ago:

- What is the unknown? What are the data? What is the condition?
- Do you know a related problem? Here is a problem related to yours and solved before. Could you use it?
- Could you restate the problem?
- Can you see clearly that each step is correct? Can you prove that it is correct?
- Can you check the result? Can you check the argument?
- Can you derive the result differently?
- Can you use the result for some other problem?

Indeed, the point of his book was to illustrate why and how such questions—which start out as the teacher's—must eventually become the students' questions whenever they confront challenging problems.

A more general point can be made here. Essential questions are not reserved only for the exploration of concepts, themes, issues, or values. Rather, as Polya's questions show, there are *process-* and *strategy*-related matters about which capable practitioners ask themselves and each other as they try to advance thought, conduct research, or improve their performance. This is why EQs are as vital in such skill areas as math, early literacy, world language, athletics, and the performing arts as they are in history or science. Success in any field depends upon learning to ask the right expert questions concerning strategy, attitude, and the meaning of the results—especially in the midst of uncertainty and confusion.

It is also worth noting that questions like Polya's are moot if there are no true problems to confront. If there is only a need to "plug and chug," then there is no need for strategy or inquiry. But in that case the education is deficient. Skills are means, not ends. The point is to learn to transfer learning and perform well in challenging situations, and that requires strategy—particularly in the face of obstacles and uncertainty (as the Polya questions highlight). Even when learning basic skills, there are endless questions (and arguments among coaches) about strategy: *which* skill to use *when,* whether in mathematics, soccer, or music.

Providing Opportunities for Intra- and Interdisciplinary Connections

Many educators seek to help students see how their learning connects within and across subjects, and essential questions provide natural and appropriate points of connection. When we refer to "appropriate points of connection," we do not mean forging intra- and interdisciplinary connections around an arbitrary theme. We have seen numerous cases in which teachers and curriculum teams, although arguably well intentioned, have produced "integrated" units that were forced, artificial, arbitrary, and superficial.

Here is a true story of one such case. A middle school team that was committed to interdisciplinary linkage designed a unit on the Victorian era. The English/ language arts teacher had students read Dickens; the social studies teacher explored tidbits of 19th century British history; and the art teacher presented paintings and sculptures from that era, and the students emulated them. But the math teacher was a holdout; she saw no point of contact in the theme for her subject and refused to play. In frustration, one of the other teachers said, "C'mon, there must be some Victorian math worth teaching!" The team ended up a bit frustrated, and mathematics was eventually given a pass. (Thankfully, science had been excluded at the outset.) Although this is a particularly egregious example of forced and arbitrary interdisciplinary connections, it serves as a cautionary tale.

It is our position that the most natural and fruitful connections are forged around transferable big ideas and companion essential questions. Suppose in this case that the unit had been framed around a few EQs, such as these: *To what extent do the arts and sciences reflect an era? Who is rich, who is poor, and why? To what extent should the wealth and influence of a country be measured? What can we learn from studying the past?* By being built around such questions, the unit would have been intellectually much richer while revealing purposeful cross-disciplinary connections (without forcing any). Note, too, that these same questions could be used in other units around other content, such as prerevolutionary France, 20th century America, and the history and economics of technological and scientific breakthroughs. Indeed, the ability or inability to apply the questions to other eras and issues is a good test of the appropriateness or arbitrariness of the proposed points of connection.

The connecting power of essential questions becomes even greater if the units are also framed by process-focused questions, such as these: *What information will best address this question? How do I find out what I don't know? How will I know what to believe in the information I find? Is there another perspective I should consider? What's the best way to show what I have learned?*

Supporting Meaningful Differentiation

A fundamental reality in teaching is that our students vary (sometimes widely) in their prior knowledge, skill levels, and experiences; in their interests; and in their preferred modes of learning and ways of showing their achievement. Even in a relatively homogeneous school the variety of abilities, interests, and needs of the learners can be substantial. Another sound reason to frame learning by essential questions has to do with this inevitable variety.

What may strike readers as ironic is that we are *not* recommending using different EQs with different groups of learners as a means of differentiation. Unlike instruction in skills, where there is a legitimate place for flexible grouping by performance levels, we propose using the same essential questions for all. Of course, it is likely that some students will consider the questions more thoughtfully or come to understandings more quickly and in greater depth. But that doesn't mean that all learners should not engage with important questions. For example, we want all primary-grade children to think about the questions *What is a number?* and *Can we put a number on everything?* as they explore the mathematical ideas of numeration. Similarly, we should engage all secondary-level students with EQs like these: *Are there descriptive limits of words? What makes a song stick in your head? When is a short answer not enough?*

Carol Ann Tomlinson, a leading expert in differentiated instruction, recommends that teachers show all of their students respect for their capacity to learn (Tomlinson & McTighe, 2006). A practical way to do this is through the regular use of EQs. By posing the *same* essential questions for a class, we signal to students that we respect their intelligence and capacity to think. The alternative would be to dumb down certain questions for lower achievers—a move that communicates diminished expectations that would likely be perceived by learners as disrespectful.

A related benefit of using the same EQs with different groups of students occurs with content instruction. Inevitably with one-size-fits-all teaching, some less able or confident learners can be confused or left behind, while more able students become bored. Framing work around essential questions can ameliorate these different reactions. Look back at the global studies example. All of the questions are accessible, and each student is likely to find at least two or three of those questions to be of interest. A constant return to those questions makes it far more likely that students who struggle with the content or have fallen behind will have multiple points of contact and "reentry" with the subject matter. And because the question, not the content, is the constant focus, even weak students could become sufficiently expert in a question or two to develop the kind of confidence and competence that they often do not feel in a typical course.

Yes, but . . .

Despite the benefits we describe and the well-documented research on the positive effects of higher-order questioning, many well-meaning teachers with whom we have worked are quick to express unease when EQs are recommended. "This is all well and good," we hear, "but we have too much content to cover to take time to engage learners in inquiry, discussion, and debate. Plus, the tests for which we are accountable do not ask such questions; and, after all, we have to prep for those tests."

With all due respect, we beg to differ. In the first place, an educator's job is not to simply *cover* content. Our role is to cause learning, not merely mention things. Our task is to *uncover* the important ideas and processes of the content so that students are able to make helpful connections and are equipped to transfer their learning in meaningful ways. If we perceive our role as fundamentally a deliverer of content, then talking fast in class is the optimal instructional method! But if we wish to engage learners in making meaning of the learning so that they come to understand it, then essential questions will serve the cause of mastery of content.

As for the concerns about accountability testing, we have long argued that such worries reflect a flawed understanding of the nature of high-stakes tests and what it takes to improve students' scores on them. It is a sad commentary on our education system when teachers feel compelled (often under pressure from myopic administrators) to practice for tests *at the expense of* more meaningful and engaged learning. Research conclusively shows that increasing the number of higher-order questions in classrooms and on local assessments significantly improves student achievement on standardized tests (Marzano, Pickering, & Pollock, 2001; Newmann, 1991). Moreover, it is false to conclude that because current accountability tests use predominantly multiple-choice items, they involve mostly low-level questions requiring recall and recognition. As analyses of test results and examinations of released items from state tests, the National Assessment of Educational Progress (NAEP), and international assessments (TIMMS, PISA) conclusively show, the most widely missed questions involve multistep reasoning and inference—*transfer,* broadly speaking. Only students who have learned to apply their learning to a novel text or problem statement can do well on such items. Coverage and rote learning will *not* improve test performance. Indeed, the often disappointing failure of test prep to improve results on standardized tests should call into question the shaky logic behind this approach.

There is no conflict, therefore, in advocating a question-based curricular framework in an accountability system that looks for specific knowledge, skill, and understanding of content. Because understanding and transfer demand active construction of meaning *by the learner,* and because long-term and flexible recall requires an intellectual framework of ideas in which to place content knowledge, only students who have learned for understanding can perform well on rigorous tests.

We trust that you now have a much better understanding of what essential questions are and why they matter in learning—the "theory" of EQs, as it were. We therefore turn in Chapter 3 to questions of practice. Where do good essential questions come from? What kinds of question might we consider for use with our particular subjects and courses? How do we design essential questions to best frame learning?

FAQ

Although test questions in reading and mathematics may require higher-order thinking and transfer (e.g., interpreting new text passages and solving multi-step word problems), most of the questions in social studies and science seem to involve recall of facts. How will the use of essential questions and inquiry prepare students for these kinds of tests?

We agree that many test questions involve recall and low-level thinking. What simply does not follow logically, however, is that "coverage" and test prep are the best ways to prepare students for such test items. This confuses cause and effect. The implied two premises in the defense of coverage are that "If I covered it, you now know it and will easily give it back on a test when prompted," and "this is therefore the most efficient preparation for tests." But these claims are unsupportable, as a moment's reflection on the better and worse performers in our own classes reveals. The student who has no mental framework, no ability to prioritize the content, and no points of connection with other previous content and experience will find initial learning difficult and long-term recall unlikely. The "coverer" is confusing the input with the output, the hope with the yield. "Teaching by mentioning" works only for the most bright, able, and motivated students.

The low yield of success from coverage is even more likely to occur if the external test questions look different than the questions used by the teacher in a local assessment. As the research on the ability to transfer makes clear, students who learned only for rote recall have little success in handling unfamiliar or novel-looking test questions.

Finally, we would note our own audits of local tests in comparison with released state tests: local assessments mimic the *format* but not the *rigor* of state assessment questions. Often, local tests, even in very high-performing districts, have a smaller percentage of higher-order questions than is found on state and national tests.

3

How Do We Design Essential Questions?

Now that you have a better understanding of the characteristics of and purposes for essential questions, we turn our attention to design. In this chapter we address the following questions: How might we come up with effective EQs for framing our units? What design strategies and tips should we keep in mind when we are generating EQs? How should we revise existing questions to make them more "essential?"

If Content Is an "Answer" . . .

One approach to developing essential questions, discussed in Chapter 1, can be seen through the following thought experiment. If the content listed in standards documents (or found in a textbook) specifies the "answers" to be learned, then what were the questions that led to those answers? For example, if learning about "three branches of government" is an outcome, what questions could help students come to understand the underlying idea and its value? How about these: *Why do we need a balance of power in government? How might we avoid abuse of power? How should leaders be "checked and balanced"?* From such general EQs, we could pose a more specific question for this topic: *Why did the Federalists advocate for a balance of power, and what were the arguments on the other side? How effective is the U.S. government's structure of three branches and what are viable alternatives?* We could also raise more general questions: *When is it wise to share power? When do we gain (and when might we lose) power by sharing it? Does balance of power inevitably lead to gridlock in government?*

The point here is straightforward—by interrogating the content in this manner, we are engaging learners in making meaning and coming to understand the content's meaning and importance. Alternately, we could have students memorize the fact that there are three branches of government and the roles of each, but how engaging and effective is that likely to be? Would such rote learning enable students to understand current and future issues related to our government? Clearly not.

Unpacking Standards to Develop Essential Questions

Essential questions can be generated from national, state, and provincial standards. Here's an efficient and effective process for "unpacking" standards. Review a set of standards and identify the key *verbs* and *nouns* that are listed (especially those nouns that recur). Often the nouns related to key verbs in declarative statements identify important concepts, and these can form the basis of an important question for students to explore. Figure 3.1 shows several examples from the Common Core State Standards in English/language arts and mathematics, and the Next Generation Standards (draft) in science, with key verbs in boldface italics and key nouns in boldface.

Figure 3.1 Unpacking Standards to Generate Essential Questions

English/LA Anchor Standards, Reading—Key Ideas and Details	Related Essential Questions
1. ***Read closely*** to ***determine*** what the **text** says explicitly and to make **logical inferences** from it; cite **specific textual evidence** when writing or speaking to support **conclusions drawn** from the text.	• What logical inferences can I draw, based on what is in the text? • What specific evidence in the text supports my ideas?
2. ***Determine* central ideas or themes** of a **text** and ***analyze*** their **development**; summarize the key **supporting details and ideas.**	• What is the central idea running through the text? • How is that idea developed? • What textual details support my argument about the central idea?
Mathematics Content Standards	**Related Essential Questions**
1. Understand **addition** as **putting together** and **adding to,** and understand **subtraction** as **taking apart** and **taking from.**	• What whole can be made from these parts? • What's left? • What should be taken away?
2. ***Define, evaluate, and compare*** functions. Use functions to ***model*** **relationships between quantities.**	• Is there a functional relationship (in response to ambiguous data)?
Mathematics Practice Standards	**Related Essential Questions**
1. ***Make sense of*** **problems** and ***persevere*** in solving them.	• What do effective problem solvers do? • What should I do when I'm stuck?
2. Use **appropriate tools** strategically.	• What is the most appropriate method and/or tool to use here, if efficiency and effectiveness are the goals? • What tool(s) will help make the work more efficient and precise?
Next Generation Science Standards	**Related Essential Questions**
1. ***Plan and carry out*** **investigations** to ***identify*** the **effect forces** have on an **object's shape and orientation.**	• Why did this move that way? • Why is this shaped that way? • What distinct forces caused that effect?

This same process can be used to analyze standards and outcomes from any source. Here are other examples of standards in the arts and physical education, respectively, with overarching and topical questions:

> **Standard:** Understanding **dance** as a way to create and communicate **meaning.** (National Art Education Association, 1994)
>
> **Overarching Essential Questions:** *How do artists best express what they think and feel? How does the medium influence the message?*
>
> **Topical Essential Questions:** *What ideas and feelings can we express through dance? How can motion convey emotion?*
>
> **Standard:** Applies movement **concepts** and **principles** to the learning and **development** of **motor skills.** (National Association for Sport and Physical Education, 2004)
>
> **Overarching Essential Questions:** *What feedback will enhance or improve performance most? What kind of practice "makes perfect"?*
>
> **Topical Essential Questions:** *How can we hit with greatest power without losing control? What will maximize distance, speed, and accuracy?*

Try your hand at unpacking standards in this way. (For more on unpacking standards, see Module I [Wiggins & McTighe, 2012] and *Understanding by Design: An Introduction* [An ASCD PD Online course].)

Deriving Essential Questions from Desired Understandings

As noted in Chapter 1, essential questions are linked to the important big ideas that we want students to come to understand. These ideas reside at the heart of all disciplines. They are timeless, cut across topics, and are embodied in *concepts* (e.g., the modern "flat" world), *themes* (e.g., love conquers all), *issues and debates* (e.g., nature versus nurture), *paradox* (e.g., poverty amidst plenty), *complex processes* (e.g., scientific isolation and control of variables), persistent *problems and challenges* (e.g., global warming), influential *theories* (e.g., manifest destiny), established *policies* (e.g., mandatory retirement age), key *assumptions* (e.g., the markets are rational), or differing *perspectives* (e.g., terrorist versus freedom fighter). These categories can be very helpful in generating possible essential questions. Figure 3.2 presents an example for the topic of nutrition.

Understandings are the specific insights, inferences, or conclusions about the big ideas that you hope your students will attain as a result of inquiry. In *Understanding by Design* (Wiggins & McTighe, 2005), we recommend that curriculum planners frame desired understandings as *full-sentence* statements—the particu-

Figure 3.2 From Concept Categories to Essential Questions for the Topic of Nutrition

Conceptual Category	Example	Essential Question
Concept	Obesity	What is an ideal weight?
Theme	A "balanced" diet	What should we eat?
Theory	Diet affects life span	How does my diet affect my life?
Policy	Government taxes or bans on sugary drinks and alcoholic beverages	Should the government have a say in what people eat and drink?
Issue/Debate	Value of synthetic vitamins and genetically altered crops	Is "natural" better?
Assumption	Three meals a day is best	How much and how often should we eat?
Perspectives	American Egg Board: "The incredible edible egg" American Heart Association: "Control cholesterol"	Whom can we believe about dietary matters?

lars of what you want learners to understand about an idea. For example, "I want my students to understand that a written constitution and encoded rule of law are essential to safeguard citizens' rights in a democracy."

Because understandings are abstractions, not facts, they are not "teachable" in the conventional sense. An understanding can be gained only through guided inference whereby the learner is helped to make, recognize, or verify a conclusion. This point suggests the critical role that essential questions play in teaching for understanding. As this book's title suggests, EQs serve to open doors to student understanding; that is, by repeatedly exploring an essential question, learners are more likely to "come to" an understanding. In other words, the EQ helps learners construct meaning out of otherwise abstract notions and disconnected facts.

Thus a straightforward way of generating essential questions is to derive them from desired understandings. Figure 3.3 shows examples from different subject areas. Of course, the reverse is true—understandings can be derived from essential questions.

Working from Overarching Questions

In the first chapter we noted that essential questions vary in size and scope and referred to the broader EQs as "overarching," in that they transcend any given unit topic and sometimes even subject areas. Although typically broader than the questions we might use to explore a specific topic, overarching questions can be very helpful for generating topical unit EQs. Look at the examples in

Figure 3.3 Essential Questions Derived from Desired Understandings

Desired Understandings	Possible Essential Questions
Great literature from various cultures explores enduring themes and reveals recurrent aspects of the human condition.	• How (much) can stories from other places and times be about us?
Statistical analysis and display often reveal patterns in data, enabling us to make predictions with degrees of confidence.	• Can you predict the future? • What will happen next? How sure are you?
Humans process both verbal and nonverbal messages simultaneously. Your communication becomes more effective when verbal and nonverbal messages are aligned.	• What makes a great speaker great? • How do great speakers use nonverbal messages?
True friendship is revealed during hard times, not happy times.	• Who is a "true friend," and how will you know?
Effective persuaders employ techniques matched to the needs, interests, and experiences of their audience. They also anticipate and rebut opposing positions.	• How can I be more persuasive?

Figure 3.4 to see how you can derive topical (unit) EQs from more general (over-arching) questions.

Here is a set of overarching essential questions in mathematics developed in Pomperaug Regional 15 School District in Middlebury, Connecticut:

• How is mathematics used to quantify and compare situations, events, and phenomena?

• What are the mathematical attributes of objects or processes, and how are they measured or calculated?

• How are spatial relationships, including shape and dimension, used to draw, construct, model, and represent real situations or solve problems?

• How is mathematics used to measure, model, and calculate change?

• What are the patterns in the information we collect, and how are they useful?

• How can mathematics be used to provide models that help us interpret data and make predictions?

• In what ways can data be expressed so that their accurate meaning is concisely presented to a specific audience?

• How do the graphs of mathematical models and data help us better understand the world in which we live?

• What do effective problem solvers do, and what do they do when they get stuck?

Once these overarching questions were identified, the math teachers found that they could fruitfully pull questions from this set to address nearly every grade-level

Figure 3.4 Deriving Topical Essential Questions from Overarching Ones

Subject	Overarching Essential Questions	Topical Essential Questions
Literature	• What makes a great story? • How do effective writers hook and hold their readers?	**Unit on mysteries** • What is unique about the mystery genre? • How do great mystery writers hook and hold their readers?
Civics/Government	• How and why do we provide checks and balances on government power?	**Unit on the U.S. Constitution** • In what ways does the Constitution attempt to limit abuse of government powers?
Visual Art	• In what ways does art shape culture as well as reflect it? • How do artists most wisely choose tools, techniques, and materials to express their ideas?	**Unit on masks** • What do masks and their use reveal about the culture? • What tools, techniques, and materials are used in creating masks from different cultures?
Science	• How does an organism's structure enable it to survive in its environment?	**Unit on insects** • How do the structure and behavior of insects enable them to survive?
Social Studies	• Why do people move?	**Unit on migration** • What factors cause today's global migrations?
Mathematics	• If axioms are like the rules of the game, which ones should we use to make the game work best, and when should we change the rules? • What differentiates a necessary and important "given" from an arbitrary "given"?	**Unit on the parallel postulate** • Should an axiom be this complex? • How important is this axiom? What makes it so important?

concept and skill. Thus they didn't have to come up with new questions for every single unit topic! Such overarching EQs can fruitfully be asked over and over again *across* the grades as they are linked to more sophisticated content. Indeed, "spiraling" the curriculum around a set of recurring questions provides the intellectual coherence needed to develop and deepen understanding of essential ideas within and across disciplines.

Overarching EQs may be developed for all subject areas. Once in place, they assist teachers in creating versions that are more topic-specific. The added benefit is for learners: by exploring these recurring questions applied to different topics across the grades, they come to "see" the larger, transferable ideas at the heart of subject matter.

Considering Possible or Predictable Misconceptions

Another fruitful source for essential questions may be found in the misconceptions that learners often harbor about subtle and abstract ideas. Experienced teachers have noticed the pattern: it is not uncommon for learners to display fundamental misunderstandings about certain concepts and skills. Moreover, there is an established body of research on students' misconceptions, particularly in science and mathematics, that can be used to generate fruitful questions. Figure 3.5 presents examples of possible misconceptions with related EQs.

Because new learning is built upon a base of prior knowledge, it is imperative that teachers use pre-assessments to ferret out potential misconceptions at the beginning of their teaching of new content. In this regard, essential questions can serve as fertile checks when employed as pre-assessments.

Considering the Facets of Understanding

In our books on Understanding by Design (Wiggins & McTighe 2005, 2011, 2012) we propose that understanding can be assessed via various facets, or indicators. We have identified six—the capacity to *explain, interpret, apply, shift perspective, empathize,* and *self-assess.* Although originally intended to serve as indicators of understanding, the facets have proven useful in generating classroom questions, including EQs. Figure 3.6 presents a set of question starters and prompting verbs based on the six facets of understanding.

Figure 3.5 Misconceptions and Related Essential Questions

Misconceptions	Possible Essential Questions
If it's written (in a textbook, in a newspaper, or in Wikipedia), it must be true.	• How do we know what to believe in what we read?
An equals sign (=) means that you have to find the answer.	• Are these values equivalent? • Is there an equivalency that can simplify this problem and help us solve it?
The scientific method is simply trial and error.	• What are the key variables that need control? • What is an efficient and effective investigation? • How can we check the validity of scientific claims?
Either you're born with ability (such as drawing, singing, good eye-hand coordination) or you're not. If you don't have natural talent, you might as well just give up.	• What makes a good artist great? • How true is it that genius is 90 percent perspiration and 10 percent inspiration (in the words of Thomas Edison)? • How can we enhance any artistic performance? • How can I improve my performance?

Figure 3.6 Question Starters, Verbs, and EQs Based on the Six Facets of Understanding

Facets of Understanding and Question Starters	Prompting Verbs	Sample EQ
Facet: Explanation		
How did _____ come about? Why is this so? What caused _____? What are the effects of _____? How might we prove/confirm/justify _____? How is _____ connected to _____? How might we help others understand _____?	• connect • demonstrate • derive • describe • design • exhibit • express • induce • instruct • justify • model • prove • show • synthesize • teach	What are causes and effects of the 9/11 attack?
Facet: Interpretation		
What is the meaning/implication of _____? What does _____ reveal about _____? How does _____ relate to me/us? So what? Why does it matter?	• create analogies • critique • illustrate • make meaning of • make sense of • provide metaphors • read between the lines • represent • tell a story of • translate	Why do they hate us? (Or is "hate" the right term?)
Facet: Application		
How and when can we use _____? How is _____ applied in the larger world? How might _____ help us to _____? What will happen next?	• adapt • build/construct • create/invent • debug • decide • design • perform • produce • propose • solve • test • use	What might prevent another 9/11? (Or can we?)

Continued on next page

Figure 3.6 *(continued)*

Facets of Understanding and Question Starters	Prompting Verbs	Sample EQ
Facet: Perspective		
What are different points of view about _____? How might this look from _____'s perspective? How is _____ similar to/different than _____? Whose story is this?	• analyze • argue • compare • contrast • critique • evaluate • infer	What is the jihadists' story of 9/11?
Facet: Empathy		
What would it be like to walk in _____'s shoes? How would you feel if you were _____? How might _____ feel about _____? What was _____ trying to make us feel/see?	• be like • be open to • believe • consider • imagine • relate • role-play • simulate	What motivates a suicide bomber?
Facet: Self-Knowledge		
What do I truly know? How do I know it? What are the limits of my knowledge about _____? Where are my "blind spots"? What are my strengths and weaknesses in _____? How are my views about _____ shaped by my (experiences, habits, prejudices, culture, etc.)?	• be aware of • realize • recognize • reflect • self-assess	In what ways did 9/11 change me or my life?

Essential Questions and Skills

Teachers with whom we have worked often find it more natural to develop essential questions for conceptual topics (e.g., themes in literature, principles of science, patterns of history) than for skill-based work (e.g., instrumental music, sports, beginning levels of world language). Indeed, we have met teachers who claim that EQs do not apply to them because "I only teach skills." Although we empathize with their concern, we do not agree with their conclusion, as we have suggested in earlier chapters.

Important ideas of purpose and strategy underlie all skill mastery, and these form the basis of fruitful essential questions, as we noted in Chapter 2 with Polya's essential questions in mathematics problem solving. In fact, considering such questions is *essential* to the ultimate goal of skill teaching—fluent and flexible performance. We have found that essential questions can be fruitfully framed around four categories of ideas relevant to effective skill learning: (1) *key concepts,* (2) *purpose and value,* (3) *strategy* and *tactics,* and (4) *context of use.*

Let's consider an example from physical education and athletics. For sports that involve the skill of swinging with long-handled objects, such as baseball, golf, lacrosse, hockey, and tennis, *key concepts* include power, torque, and control. Thus, as we have suggested, we might frame a question for exploring these ideas, such as "How does torque affect power?" Or more generally, we could pose the question "How can you hit with greatest power without losing control?" to help learners develop effective *strategies* for their swings (e.g., keeping eyes on the ball or puck and follow-through). A third question relates to *context:* "When should we swing softly?"

The same categories are useful in academic skill areas, such as reading: *How do you know that you comprehend what you are reading?* (key concept); *How important is it for readers to regularly monitor their comprehension?* (purpose and value); *What do good readers do when they don't understand the text?* (strategy); and *When should we use "fix-up" strategies?* (context of use). Figure 3.7 presents additional examples of possible essential questions to use when teaching skills.

As noted in the previous chapters, intent is everything when judging the essentialness of questions. Thus, to engender genuine inquiry as opposed to only posing leading questions in skills-focused work, questions related to strategy and value have to arise from the kinds of problems or challenges in which such strategic decisions must be made.

Accordingly, questions in skill areas are essential only when asked in a context of genuine performance challenges, where ongoing judgments and adjustments are required. In real-world skills applications, rote learning will rarely suffice. Skills are means, not ends, and their aim is *transfer*—fluent, flexible, and effective performance in varying contexts. That outcome requires the ability to make wise choices from a repertoire—that is, understanding *which* skill to use *when, how,* and *why,* when confronted with complex performance challenges.

Revising Essential Questions

Developing good essential questions is not easy. Even experienced teachers who possess a deep knowledge of their subjects have exclaimed that crafting EQs is tough. As Jerome Bruner (1960) famously put it: "Given particular subject matter or a particular concept, it is easy to ask trivial questions. . . . It is also easy to ask impossibly difficult questions. The trick is to find the medium questions that can be answered and that take you somewhere" (p. 40).

Indeed, the ability to generate good essential questions is a learned skill, and very few people create a perfect EQ on the first try. We have found it helpful to think of designing essential questions as a genre of writing, and like the writing process itself, it typically requires drafts, feedback, and revisions.

A basic tip for reviewing and revising EQs is to evaluate them against the seven defining characteristics presented in Chapter 1. Also, show your draft questions to

Figure 3.7 Skills, Strategies, and Related Essential Questions

Subject	Skills	Strategies	Related EQs
Reading	"Sound out" unfamiliar words.	Use context clues to figure out the word's meaning.	• What is the author trying to say? • How can I infer or find out what these words might mean?
Writing	Follow the five-paragraph essay structure.	Match your word choices with your purpose and audience.	• How can I best achieve my purpose with this audience?
Mathematics	Dividing fractions: Invert and multiply.	Problem solving: • Simplify equivalent expressions. • Work backward from end result.	• How can I turn unknowns into knowns? • What is the most revealing final form?
Visual Arts/Graphic Design	Use the color wheel to select complementary colors.	Use colors to reinforce the mood you want to evoke in the viewer.	• What am I trying to make the viewer feel? • How can I best express it?
Carpentry	Apply proper techniques when using a band saw.	Measure twice, cut once.	• How can I best save time, money, and energy?
Instrumental Music and Keyboarding	Practice to achieve automaticity in skill performance.	To make practice time most effective, one must have clear goals, constantly monitor performance, seek and heed feedback, and make needed adjustments.	• If practice makes perfect, what makes perfect practice?

other teachers (especially those who understand EQs) for feedback. In curriculum planning, it's easy to become too close to your work or to get writer's block, and sometimes all it takes is another set of eyes to spark a breakthrough.

The bad news: as noted, writing essential questions that meet our criteria is not easy. The good news: this is a skill that improves with practice. To help you build this skill set, study the sets of "before and after" essential questions in Figure 3.8 to see examples of revisions and associated comments.

Did you notice what is common to the revisions? They move away from the convergent toward more open and nuanced questions. The revised versions imply that there is a range of plausible answers or that a thoughtful judgment has to be made. They call for inquiry and extended thinking, and answers are likely to be refined or even rethought as understanding deepens. Note that although the original questions could certainly be used as part of a study of a given topic, they are not the best for framing the whole inquiry.

You also may have noticed that there are some simple techniques for opening up the question: *To what extent? How well? How much?* These small but helpful edits now make more clear that there is a *range* of possible answers, not just a single right answer.

Of course, the best test of an essential question comes in its use. Does it in fact engage the learners in productive inquiry? Does it stimulate thinking, discussion, and even debate? Does it spark rethinking and further questions? Does it lead to deeper insights about important matters? If not, revisions are needed. If so, your question has realized its promise.

FAQs

How many essential questions and companion understandings should a unit have?

The answer depends in large part on the scope and time frame of the unit. A 2-week unit on a specific topic within one subject area would likely have fewer EQs and understandings than a 12-week interdisciplinary unit. That said, we typically see between two and four essential questions in a unit of 3 to 4 weeks' duration. The important thing to remember is that quality, not quantity, counts. It does not follow that a unit with more targeted essential questions (and related understandings) is better than a unit with fewer. In this regard, it is useful to invoke a variation of the Marine Corps recruiting motto: We seek "only a few good" inquiries. If they are truly essential, they can (and should) establish priorities and help uncover the key ideas. Do not state questions that you do not intend to actively pursue through discussion, research, problem solving, and other constructivist means. Finally, keep in mind that a truly essential question is one that we will continually revisit throughout the unit, so we don't want too many. The same is

Figure 3.8 Revising Essential Questions

Original Question	Comment on the Draft	Revised Question	Comment on the Revision
What is nonfiction?	This is a definitional question that can be answered unambiguously.	**How much license does a writer of nonfiction have to make a point?**	This version explores an interesting gray area with both historical and contemporary relevance.
How does this diet match up with the government's nutritional guidelines?	The question requires some analysis and evaluation, but it can be answered "correctly."	**What should we eat?**	This is much more open, with lots of potential for inquiry and debate.
Are there any benefits from the deforestation of the rain forests?	The question calls for some information gathering and analysis, but it results in a list.	**To what extent do the costs outweigh the benefits of deforestation of the rain forests?**	The revision broadens and deepens the inquiry, calling for more sophisticated analysis; it's more likely to spark debate and deeper inquiry into a list of pros and cons.
Who speaks Spanish in our community?	This is a nonproblematic question asking for a list (although some inquiry may be required).	**How well can you thrive in our community speaking only English?**	The revision is more provocative, calling for greater analysis and a shift of perspective.
Is your answer accurate?	This question calls for a straightforward answer.	**Is your answer appropriately precise for this situation?**	The revision is more open and gets at how the context determines the appropriate degree of precision.
What distinguishes Impressionist art?	This is a leading question with an expected set of characteristics.	**Why and how do artists break with tradition? What are the effects?**	These questions require an examination of artistic trends and a learner generalization.
What types of exercises will improve fitness?	This question involves research but is leading: the answers are straightforward.	**"No pain, no gain"—agree?**	The revision is more provocative, likely to spark discussion and debate.

true with understandings: these should reflect transferable "big ideas," thus we need only a few.

Should there be an essential question for each identified understanding?

Although we do not necessarily seek a one-to-one correspondence, there should be a clear connection between the EQs and the understandings. Think of the essential questions as doorways for exploring the big ideas, leading to the desired understandings. Thus if you identify one or more important understandings in a unit, you should have one or more companion EQs. A simple test is to draw connecting lines between the targeted understandings and related EQs on the UbD unit-planning template (see Wiggins & McTighe, 2005, 2011). A "free-floating" understanding or EQ signals the need to add (or drop) one or the other to bring the two categories into alignment.

4

How Do We Use Essential Questions?

Now that you have a better sense of the characteristics of essential questions and ways of designing them, we turn to the question of implementation. How should essential questions be put into action to ensure meaningful student engagement, persistent inquiry, thoughtful deliberation, and the necessary rethinking to lead to understanding?

In this chapter, we explore practical tips and techniques for helping you get the most from your essential questions. And although in Chapter 6 we will engage in a detailed exploration of ways to establish a "culture of inquiry" in your classroom, we need to comment on its importance here as a key to successful implementation.

No initiative, practice, or policy is guaranteed to succeed. As with any seed to be planted, the soil must be ready and conducive to growth. The seedbed of education involves the beliefs, values, structures, routines, protocols, and climate that influence actions, shape attitudes, and affect learning. A healthy culture is one in which everyone shares aims and acts in concert to advance them.

The seed and seedbed analogy is important in another sense. Many of the best student comments in response to challenging questions are tentative, glib, or naïve. Thus every response is like a seedling with potential that needs nurturing and sometimes pruning. Similarly, the sharing and refinement of burgeoning ideas can happen only in a climate that supports intellectual risk taking. On the other hand, the culture has to be built on a commitment of sound evidence and reasoning in which any opinion without proper reasoning and supportive evidence becomes recognized as lacking. So if we value open yet disciplined inquiry, if we seek thoughtful, not thoughtless, responses to questions, then we must shape the environment accordingly. That shaping requires us to ensure a safe and inviting space for thinking out loud while also making clear that certain habits, beliefs, actions, and contributions can undermine the aim of free thought and collaborative inquiry.

New Rules

The importance of thinking explicitly about a culture that supports inquiry comes from the fact that a focus on essential questions establishes new rules for the game called school. For the majority of learners, school is a place where the teacher has the answers and classroom questions are intended to find out who knows them. Ironically, many teachers signal that this is the game even when they don't intend to communicate it—for example, by posing questions that elicit only a yes/no or single right answer, by calling only on students with raised hands, and by answering their own questions after a brief pause.

We acknowledge that these can be difficult habits to break. Indeed, noteworthy research conducted in conjunction with the Trends in International Mathematics and Science Study (TIMSS) revealed how different approaches to questioning can take root and escape our notice. When the first TIMSS studies compared instructional practices in U.S. and Japanese classrooms, the authors noted an important difference in beliefs that played out in classroom behavior and lesson plans:

> Teachers ask questions for different reasons in the United States and in Japan. In the United States, the purpose of a question is to get an answer. In Japan, teachers pose questions to stimulate thought. A Japanese teacher considers a question to be a poor one if it elicits an immediate answer, for this indicates that students were not challenged to think. One teacher we interviewed told us of discussions she had with her fellow teachers on how to improve teaching practices. "What do you talk about?" we wondered. "A great deal of the time," she reported, "is spent talking about questions we can pose to the class—which wordings work best to get students involved in thinking and discussing the material. One good question can keep a whole class going for a long time; a bad one produces little more than a simple answer." (Stevenson & Stigler, 1992, p. 195)

All successful implementation starts with clear and explicit goals. And because the goal of EQs is different than the goal of content acquisition, this principle is all the more critical. It must therefore become clear that when essential questions are on the table, the aim is sustained inquiry and rich discussion increasingly facilitated by students, not a hunt for *the* answer that the teacher thinks is correct.

In addition to confronting deeply held (and often unexamined) beliefs and comfortable habits by teachers, the implementation of EQs requires a deliberate effort to reorient students to the new rules of the game. We recommend discussing *explicitly* the purpose, associated practices, and changed roles that the use of essential questions entails. Here are some examples of key ideas to communicate that may prepare students for the changes:

- There's not a single correct answer for this question. Life is about the consideration of plausible and imperfect alternatives.
- Everyone is entitled to an opinion, but the best opinions are supported by valid evidence and sound reasons.
- Coming to understand important ideas is like attaining fitness: it takes work and practice over time.
- When a question is posted on the wall, it means that we are going to consider it again and again.
- Inquiry is not a spectator sport; each person needs to listen actively and participate.
- Everyone is fair game. I won't only call on people who raise their hands.
- If and when I or others challenge your comment, it doesn't mean we don't like you or don't value your contribution. We're testing the strength of the idea.
- Considering another point of view in an open-minded way might help you clarify and expand your thinking and understanding.
- Making mistakes is an expected part of learning. If you never risk making a mistake, you're not likely to improve. That's why we question answers—in order to improve them.
- You may find that you are reconsidering things that you thought you understood. That is normal—even desirable.

Like the care of seedlings, the new rules will require patience, careful nurturing, and constant reminders. Over time, the new rules will become the norms, allowing big ideas to take root and mature understandings to blossom.

A Four-Phase Process for Implementing Essential Questions

The most obvious way in which implementation of essential questions differs from conventional instruction is that the question is not just asked, discussed, and left behind as different content is covered. The whole point of the essential question specifically (and teaching for understanding more generally) is that the exploration is designed to be spiral-like or flow back and forth between the question and new sources of information, experience, or perspective. In other words, we need to repeatedly return to the question to probe further, think more deeply, and arrive at more insightful understandings.

We can describe what has to happen in any successful use of EQs, then, in terms of a four-phase process:

Phase 1: Introduce a question designed to cause inquiry.

Goal: Ensure that the EQ is thought-provoking, relevant to both students and the content of the current unit or course, and explorable via text, a research project, a lab, a problem, an issue, or a simulation in which the question comes to life.

Phase 2: Elicit varied responses and question those responses.

Goal: Use questioning techniques and protocols as necessary to elicit the widest possible array of different *plausible, yet imperfect* answers to the question. Also, probe the original question in light of the different takes on it that are implied in the varied student answers and due to inherent ambiguity in the words of the question.

Phase 3: Introduce and explore new perspectives.

Goal: Bring new text, data, or phenomena to the inquiry, designed to deliberately extend inquiry or call into question tentative conclusions reached thus far. Elicit and compare new answers to previous answers, looking for possible connections and inconsistencies to probe.

Phase 4: Reach tentative closure.

Goal: Ask students to generalize their findings, new insights, and remaining (or newly raised) questions into provisional understandings about both content and process.

Note that this process is not restricted to a single unit. We can use this framework to string different units together so that Phase 3 could be the start of a new unit in which a novel perspective is introduced and explored using the same question or questions.

Here is a simple example from science using the question "What is science?" In many middle school and high school science courses, teachers often devote an *initial* unit or lesson to the question. Typically, though, after an early reading and discussion, the question is dropped, never to return that year as attention turns to acquiring specific knowledge and skill. (This pattern is aided and abetted by most textbooks.) Let's see how the framework helps us more clearly see an alternative approach in which the essential question becomes more prominent throughout the course.

Phase 1: Introduce a question designed to cause inquiry.

Example: *What is science? How does it relate to or differ from common sense and religious views on empirical issues?*

Phase 2: Elicit varied responses and question those responses.

Example: Students read three different short documents or excerpts that address the EQ, in which there is great disagreement about what science is, how it works, and how much stock we should put in its answers.

Phase 3: Introduce and explore new perspectives (in this case, several times during the year).

Example: Students are asked to perform two different experiments in which methods vary and margin of error is salient. They also read about a few controversies and false discoveries in the history of science (e.g., read work by Karl Popper on how science is inherently testable and tentative—"falsifiable"—where political, social, and religious ideology can always explain anything; read work by Richard Feynman on how most people misunderstand what science is; read work by David Hume on why we should be inherently skeptical about science as truth).

Phase 4: Reach tentative closure.

Example: Ask students to generalize their findings, new insights, and remaining (or newly raised) questions about the nature of science.

As the example suggests, proper treatment of the question would demand not only that the question be *constantly* revisited throughout the year—"Based on the previous two experiments and lively disagreements about the findings in the research on global warming, what would you *now* say science is?"—but also that the course must include a look at pseudo-science and the danger of confirmation bias. In addition, the course should consider the very *counterintuitive* aspects of modern scientific thinking (which often give rise to common and persistent student misconceptions in the sciences and about science itself).

The same failure to revisit a few key ideas around essential questions occurs far too frequently in mathematics. Arguably the most common and unfortunate mistake occurs when whatever is proposed as "givens"—the definitions, rules, axioms—is only briefly discussed in an introductory unit and then never revisited. The textbook proposes some assumptions, rarely argues for them, and then rushes off to prove things based on them. But why *those* assumptions? Why *can't* we define basic terms? What *is* a number? These questions naturally arise yet are quickly and subtly smothered by conventional texts and teaching.

To ignore these questions is an error of both pedagogy and mathematical understanding. In fact, it was only by constantly considering the essential question "What are we assuming and are we right to assume it?" that modern mathematics was born. For example, until Descartes, no one assumed that there could be numbers to the 4th power (e.g., x^4) because the exponents supposedly referred to spatial dimensions—which is why we call x^2 "x squared" and x^3 "x cubed"! Student-led inquiry into axioms and the development of one's own theory of space formed the basis of the most famous experiment in the teaching of geometry, developed by Harold Fawcett in the 1930s and found in his book *The Nature of Proof* (1938).

Indeed, the elegance and power of mathematics only really come to life when we engage learners in intellectually rich questions such as these: *Why can't you divide by zero when you can multiply by zero? Why would we have something so counterintuitive as negative or "imaginary" numbers? Why do we assume the parallel postulate when it is neither self-evident nor simple to state? Who introduced these ideas, and with what reasons?* Modern arithmetic, geometry, algebra, and calculus all derive from such inquiries that compel us back to essential questions. For example, the introduction of zero into the number system came fairly late in the game and was viewed as highly controversial. (For a fascinating and readable account of the great historical controversies and innovations in math, read *Euclid's Window* by Leonard Mlodinow.) Thus a proper handling of the question of what can and cannot be accepted as axiomatic must involve a *constant* revisiting after milestones have been reached (e.g., the proof that the angles in any triangle equal 180 degrees, the Pythagorean theorem, pseudo-proofs such as 1 = 0 that rely on a zero divisor). For it was such a constant *rethinking* of givens that led to alternate geometries, calculus, probability theory, and Einstein's theory of relativity.

With younger children, an inquiry into "givens" can intriguingly begin by a close look at a simpler analogous case: the rules of familiar games. Here are some questions to consider: *Why assume* those *rules? Why can't two runners occupy the same base at the same time in baseball? Why is there a three-point shot in basketball, and how far should it be from the basket, and why have various rules committees changed the distance over the years? Can some rules be changed to* improve *the game without really* changing *it?* For example, in the case of the last question, why not change the current rule in baseball so that a fouled third strike bunt attempt would be treated as a foul ball (still at bat) instead of as it is now, as a third strike (out)? This can lead to in-depth consideration of why some axioms are developed *after the fact* to make the "game" work *the way we want it to*—a noteworthy and unobvious understanding that is important in the history of geometry and routinely ignored in textbook treatment of axioms.

Here's an example of how our four-phase EQ process could be used in an inquiry into "givens" in secondary mathematics:

Phase 1: Introduce a question designed to cause inquiry.

Example: In math, *given* what is given: What is essential and what is merely conventional? Why is it given? Who *gave* it and why do you think it wise to assume it? What distinguishes a vital foundation from a changeable convention? Look at other givens in our lives, such as the Bill of Rights, the meaning of essential words in dictionaries, or budget assumptions.

Phase 2: Elicit varied responses and question those responses.

Example: Start with the rules of games, laws, or language, and then bridge to mathematics. Ask students to look at questionable givens. For example, we can't define a line or point, but we still draw them a certain way; we can't divide by zero, but we can multiply by zero; we use a base 10 system but we often use the binary system; we use PEMDAS in algebra to unpack statements, but couldn't we use another convention? Is the commutative property equally conventional?

Phase 3: Introduce and explore new perspectives.

Example: Briefly consider other geometries (e.g., "taxicab" geometry, the geometry of city grids) to illustrate why it is valuable to make different assumptions about spatial relationships, depending on context. Look at false proofs that play off some of these givens, or consider other assumptions to see why they might or might not be wise. For example, have students look at what happens if we assume that all lines are curved, as in spherical geometry and modern physics.

Phase 4. Reach tentative closure.

Example: Ask students to look back at the arithmetic, algebra, or geometry axioms proposed in the textbook and generalize their findings, new insights, and remaining (or newly raised) questions about what we should and should not assume without proof; and which givens are foundational and which are conventional.

Here is another example of these four phases applied to an elementary social studies unit on regions. Notice how the unit plan reflects a similar kind and flow of inquiry as in the mathematics example. These EQs are introduced: *Why are North, South, East, and West and the like accepted as givens when talking about regions? Are other regional distinctions perhaps as helpful?*

Phase 1: Introduce a question designed to cause inquiry.

Example: After a cursory lesson on the typical names and characteristics of U.S. regions, ask these questions: *Could we carve up the map differently? What kinds of regions might be just as useful for us to define? What regions might we also be said to live in? How many regions do we live in?*

Phase 2: Elicit varied responses and question those responses.

Example: *To what extent is defining an area as a "region" useful?* Compare and contrast the benefits and weaknesses of various regional maps and categories for school, town, and state; and alternate regions of the United States, based on cultural aspects (such as regional sports affiliations).

Phase 3: Introduce and explore new perspectives.

Example: Pursue the idea of regions based on cultural aspects (food, leisure, jobs) and thus the extent to which talking about regions like "the South" or "the Northwest" may be unhelpful because it can cause us to stereotype and overlook uniqueness or diversity in every region. Related questions can then be explored: *To what extent do we usefully define ourselves in "regional" terms—for example, Southerner, coastal, West Tennessee, upstate New York, Northern California—as opposed to by state or nation? When is it useful to define a region by physical characteristics and when is it useful to define it by sociological characteristics?*

Phase 4: Reach tentative closure.

Example: Ask students to generalize their findings, new insights, and remaining (or newly raised) questions about regions and the usefulness of the idea.

Let's now look at an expanded version of the framework, beginning with a consideration of how content and inquiry will be blended, and what resources (beyond the textbook) may be needed to shape the inquiry. And, of course, we will want to conclude with some formal assessment of student understanding during and after the inquiry—the kind of assessment that is almost never called for in textbook chapter tests.

An Eight-Phase Process for Implementing Essential Questions

A finer-grained implementation of EQs can be described in eight phases: (1) pre-instructional planning and design, (2) initial posing of the question, (3) eliciting of varied student responses, (4) probing of those responses (and of the question itself), (5) introduction of new information and perspectives on the question, (6) in-depth and sustained inquiry culminating in products or performance, (7) tentative closure, and (8) assessment of individual student inquiry and answers.

Phase 1: Pre-instructional planning and design.

Goal: Given the EQ, assemble relevant but diverse texts, problems, or experiences to be used to extend and deepen inquiry.

Phase 2: Initial posing of the question.

Goal: Propose the EQ either at the start or after an initial investigation relevant to the question.

Phase 3: Eliciting of varied student responses.

Goal: Ensure that the students understand that multiple plausible answers are likely and that the selected resources are highly likely to give rise to such differences of opinion.

Phase 4: Probing of those responses (and the question itself).

Goal: Question student responses; point out inconsistencies or disagreements when all responses are considered; invite students to propose directions or methods of further inquiry. Ensure that the question itself is reconsidered and analyzed in light of the responses.

Phase 5: Introduction of new information and perspectives on the question.

Goal: Bring new text, data, or phenomena to the inquiry, designed to deliberately further open up inquiry or call into question tentative conclusions reached thus far.

Phase 6: In-depth and sustained inquiry culminating in products or performance.

Goal: Students are expected, whether individually, in small groups, or as a class, to explore the EQ and the most promising responses via an in-depth investigation and discussion that is shared and analyzed.

Phase 7: Tentative closure.

Goal: The class summarizes its findings, new insights, and remaining (or new) questions—about both content and process.

Phase 8: Assessment of individual student inquiry and answers.

Goal: Students individually must formally explain their current answer to the question, supported by evidence and logic while also addressing counterevidence and counterargument.

Let's return to the example in Chapter 2 from Grant's English teaching to see how these phases play out. The unit essential question was "Who sees and who is blind?" The preselected readings for this EQ were Hans Christian Andersen's "The Emperor's New Clothes," "Winnie the Pooh and Piglet Hunt Woozles" (a chapter from *Winnie the Pooh*), *Oedipus the King,* and Plato's "Allegory of the Cave" from *The Republic* (though, obviously, any readings could be used that are appropriate for both reading level and the issues related to the question).

Students are given the essential question on the first day of the unit. They are strongly encouraged to take notes around the EQ and related questions that will arise as inquiry unfolds. They know that the readings relate to the questions. And they know that the EQ will appear as an essay on the final assessment. In short, the unit design, framed around the essential question, clearly presents the challenge, and the work throughout the unit is focused accordingly. Here is how the unit unfolds in terms of the eight phases:

Phase 1: Pre-instructional planning and design.

Example: Choose four texts of varied difficulty that bear on the EQ and provide different perspectives on it.

Phase 2: Initial posing of the question.

Example: Start with a brief discussion of personal "blindness" in one's life— examples and brief discussion of causes for not "seeing" what was clearly there to be "seen." Teacher then introduces EQ and first reading: "Winnie the Pooh and Piglet Hunt Woozles."

Phase 3: Eliciting of varied student responses.

Example: Who sees and who is blind in the story segment? Are some more blind than others here (e.g., Piglet versus Pooh, Pooh versus Christopher Robin in the tree above)? Why?

Phase 4: Probing of those responses (and the question itself).

Example: How do these ideas relate to your personal accounts from the previous activity? What does *blind* really mean? What does *see* really mean here? What is the moral of the story in terms of blindness, then? Can we make some initial generalizations about blindness and vision to be further explored in later readings?

Phase 5: Introduction of new information and perspectives on the question.

Example: Read "The Emperor's New Clothes," *Oedipus the King,* or "The Allegory of the Cave." Watch clips from *The Matrix, Twilight Zone,* or the scene in *The Miracle Worker* in which Helen Keller links water to the sign for water. Other possibilities include nonfiction accounts of sight/blindness, perceptual bias, the research on cognitive bias and error, and other related topics.

Phase 6: In-depth and sustained inquiry culminating in products or performance.

Example: Use the same or similar questions to explore each text or a real-world case study in greater depth, getting at the paradoxes in the answer. (Note that in "The

Emperor's New Clothes," the *child* sees, not the *expert*; the blind man sees in *Oedipus;* the experts and academically successful are blind in the cave; and so on.)

Phase 7: Tentative closure.

Example: Create a comprehensive diagram to compare and contrast the answers to the question suggested by the texts and by students.

Phase 8: Assessment of individual student inquiry and answers.

Example: Write an essay on "Who sees and who is blind?" in which you weave together what we have read with your own ideas and experience, to make a compelling and interesting argument. Also, propose a museum exhibit for inclusion in a show devoted to the essential question.

Note that in this case, the EQ can also naturally transcend the boundaries of English to encompass history (*Why is there mass hysteria, self-destructive fascism, patriotic blindness?*), science (*Why is Darwinian evolution or global warming viewed as dangerous by otherwise reasonable people?*), the arts (*Why does art threaten? Why do some people view modern art as a fraud?*), and athletics (*How do pitchers deceive batters, and players deceive referees? What do the great players "see" in the midst of a game that other players do not see, and why?*).

In other words, understanding by *design,* not mere teacher questioning, makes an EQ come to life and go into depth. The texts, prompts, rules of engagement, and final assessments provide the key elements needed for the learning design to succeed, in light of the just-noted criteria: an intriguing question (especially to adolescents who are often painfully aware of wisdom, folly, and blindness in their midst, if only in the adults and in peers!), inherent ambiguity, clearly different points of view, and many shades of gray that will require careful questioning of ideas and close reading of the text.

Are you thinking that this approach is too sophisticated for younger students? If so, consider this example using the same framework for elementary students on the essential question "Who is a true friend?"

Phase 1: Pre-instructional planning and design.

Example: Choose three texts of varied difficulty that bear on the EQ and provide different perspectives on it (e.g., *Frog and Toad Are Friends* or *Charlotte's Web*).

Phase 2: Initial posing of the question.

Example: Start with a brief discussion of friendship in one's life—examples and reasons: Who are your friends? What makes them your friends?

Phase 3: Eliciting of varied student responses.

Example: Ask, "What can we say in general makes someone a friend or not a friend?" Prepare a T-chart to summarize answers.

Phase 4: Probing of those responses (and the question itself).

Example: Is a friend only someone you just hang with or see every day? What does "best friend forever" (BFF) really mean?

Phase 5: Introduction of new information and perspectives on the question.

Example: Read the "Spring" section of *Frog and Toad Are Friends* and discuss friendship and lying. For example, Does a true friend lie to a friend? Are there other things that Frog and Toad each do to one another that seem "unfriendly"? Does it still make sense to call them friends? Is there a difference between a normal friend and a *true* friend?

Phase 6: In-depth and sustained inquiry culminating in products or performance.

Example: Use the same or similar questions to explore *Charlotte's Web*.

Phase 7: Tentative closure.

Example: So, who is a true friend and why? Create a Venn diagram to compare and contrast the answers to the question suggested by the text and by students.

Phase 8: Assessment of individual student inquiry and answers.

Example: Choose one of the following:

- Make a booklet to teach others how to know if someone is a true friend.
- Pretend to "order" a true friend from a friendship website.
- Create a "want ad" for a true friend. What characteristics do you want?

Such a framework, then, can help us think through the needed elements and sequence in unit design that advance in-depth inquiry. This "thinking through" is vital because typical lesson plans that derive from the textbook or coverage rarely include the kind of shifts of perspective and deepening of discourse so central to true inquiry. (Note: Do not fixate on the number of phases or every detail of the indicators proposed; the framework is simply a device for helping you work through instructional design more thoughtfully.)

Response Strategies

Such frameworks for working with EQs, although necessary, are not sufficient. The key to getting the most from your EQs rests in the use of follow-up questions and subsequent learning activities. Here is a set of practical and proven techniques for engaging more learners and extending their thinking and meaning-making. Although these methods may be employed with most types of classroom questions, they are especially effective when used in conjunction with open-ended questions that do not have a "correct" or expected answer.

Wait Time

"Wait time" refers to the period of teacher silence that follows the posing of a question (Wait Time I), as well as that following an initial student response (Wait Time II). Extensive research on wait time has confirmed several benefits of using this simple technique (Rowe, 1974; Tobin & Capie, 1980; Tobin, 1984):

- The length of student responses increased.
- More frequent, unsolicited contributions (relevant to the discussion) were made.

- An increase in the logical consistency of students' explanations occurred.
- Students voluntarily increased the use of evidence to support inferences.
- The incidence of speculative responses increased.
- The number of questions asked by students increased.
- Greater participation by "slower" learners occurred.

These results have been validated at the elementary, middle, high school, and college levels. In terms of teacher behavior, the following changes resulted from the regular use of the wait time technique:

- The use of higher-level, evaluative questions increased.
- The percentage of "teacher talk" decreased.
- Teachers demonstrated greater response flexibility.
- Teachers' expectations for the performance of students rated as "slow learners" improved.

In terms of Wait Time II (waiting after a student responds), when teachers do not respond immediately to a student's response, the student is more likely to elaborate or support the answer given (or change it), and other students are implicitly invited to chime in.

Think-Pair-Share

One practical and effective means of implementing wait time in the classroom has been developed by Dr. Frank Lyman (1981) and his colleagues. This strategy, known as Think-Pair-Share (TPS), structures time to think into a multimode cycle. In this cycle, students *listen* to a question or presentation, which is followed by individual quiet *think* time. During this period students are not permitted to converse or to raise their hands to respond. However, they are encouraged to write down or diagram their thoughts. At a designated time, signaled by the teacher, students form *pairs* and exchange thoughts with their partner. The pairing period is then followed by a *sharing* session, often in the form of a class discussion. Think-Pair-Share combines the well-documented effects of wait time with the cognitive and affective benefits of cooperative learning, all within an easily managed classroom routine. TPS enables each student to actively engage with the question, while allowing shy or less confident students an opportunity to rehearse their response in a safe space before responding in front of the entire class and the teacher.

Random Calling

We strongly recommend that teachers abandon the habit of calling only on students who raise their hands to respond to a question. (In fact, over time you will want students to stop raising their hands at all, as in normal human discourse.) The alternatives are random calling, whereby every pupil has an equal chance of being invited to respond (e.g., via drawing names from a fishbowl), or targeted calling, where you make clear that everyone is expected to be ready to say something, and those who regularly speak will sometimes be overlooked for a period of time. Although the procedure of calling on students randomly or purposefully in these ways might seem rather simple and straightforward, it goes against long-standing classroom habits and familiar roles—for both learners and their instructors. (A particularly clear and practical account of this technique can be found in Lemov, 2010.) Researcher Dylan Wiliam (2007/2008), an advocate of random calling, tells an illustrative story about the challenge of changing comfortable instructional practices, especially for veterans:

> A few months ago, an elementary school teacher . . . was telling me about her efforts to change her questioning techniques. She wanted to use popsicle sticks with students' names on them as a way of choosing students to answer her questions at random—a technique that increases student engagement and elicits answers from a broad range of students instead of just the usual suspects. However, she was having difficulty calling on specific students because she automatically started most questions with phrases like, "Does anyone know . . . ?" Frustrated, she wondered why she was finding this simple change so difficult. This teacher has been teaching for 25 years, and we worked out that, over her career, she has probably asked around half a million questions. When you've done something one way half a million times, doing it another way is going to be pretty difficult! (p. 38)

A switch to "cold calling" can be challenging for students as well as for teachers. You may initially experience pushback from students as familiar and comfortable pedagogical norms are altered. Nonetheless, persistence in the face of objections will establish the "new rules" of your classroom; that is, everyone is fair game and expected to be attentive and participate.

A variation of this technique is "student calling," whereby the teacher asks a student to select another student to respond ("Marion, will you please call on someone else to reply?"). In our experience, students will often call on their friends—or sometimes their enemies! Either way, this method stirs the pot and keeps everyone on their toes. More important, it sets the stage for greater autonomy by learners in initiating and executing a collaborative inquiry.

Yet another method to promote active listening among students is to periodically ask students to summarize what has been said, as in, "Justin, could you please summarize Maria's point?" Then check back with the originator: "Maria, did Justin accurately capture your idea?" Regular use of this technique sets up a desirable outcome related to autonomy; that is, students begin to take ownership of clarifying and restating contributions. (These ideas are explored more fully in the upcoming section on Socratic seminars, p. 61.)

Class Survey

By using several methods for all-pupil response, teachers can involve an entire class in responding to questions. Perhaps the simplest way is to have students use hand signals, such as thumbs up, thumbs down. For example, "Do you agree with the author's contention that . . . ?" The responses open the door for further probing ("Why do you think that?"), debate ("Roberto, tell us why you disagree with Alexis"), and paired discussion of opposite-minded people ("Pick someone who had the opposite view and explain your position").

Some teachers ask students to use small whiteboards to record brief responses to questions and prompts. Although this method tends to be more commonly used to check for knowledge, sometimes the boards can work with more open-ended questions. For example, a college history professor asks, "Which 20th century U.S. president will have the most disappointing legacy? Be prepared to say why." Imagine a class full of students holding up their varied answers—and the ensuing debates!

As in most walks of life these days, inexpensive technology is available to assist. In this case, wireless polling of students can be easily managed using student-response systems, informally known as clickers. These small devices allow teachers to get an immediate response from all class members and display the results immediately on a computer or tablet. Cell phones can now be used for the same purpose. Whether high- or low-tech, the regular use of these survey techniques changes classroom dynamics by counteracting student passivity as well as dominance by those who happily talk in class all the time.

More Than One Answer

As we have noted, effective essential questions are inherently open—designed to spark discussion and, often, debate. Accordingly, teachers should be careful not to stop once a thoughtful inference or seemingly solid conclusion is attained. We encourage teachers to push for at least two or three *different* answers, as suggested in Phase 2 of the four-part framework previously described. Then probe to invite comparisons and testing of the various ideas on the table. The absence of different plausible responses or perspectives can be a telltale sign that your EQ is too narrow or so abstract or vague that students are unable to offer differing points of view.

Probes for Thinking and Support

The value of probing questions has long been recognized as the key element of a Socratic dialogue, and research confirms their value (Krupa, Selman, & Jaquette, 1985). However, research also points out that the use of probing questions is an infrequent practice in many classrooms (Newmann, 1988). Teachers can use probing questions, such as "Why?" "Can you elaborate?" and "What evidence can you present to support your answer?" to press students to consider and weigh diverse evidence, to examine the validity of their deductions and inductions, to consider opposing points of view, and to encourage "unpacking" of their thinking to reveal how they have reached particular conclusions. Probing questions ask students to extend their knowledge beyond factual recall and parroting of learned answers, to apply what is known to what is unknown, and to elaborate on what is known to deepen their understanding of this knowledge.

Probing follow-up questions are "essential" when using EQs and other open-ended queries to push students' thinking and meaning-making. Here are examples of familiar probes:

- What do you mean by _____?
- Why?
- Can you elaborate? Tell me more.
- Could you rephrase that? I don't understand your point.
- Could you give me an example or an analogy to explain that?
- How does this relate to (what we said before; what we read last week)?
- Can we come up with another perspective on this?
- What are you assuming when you say that?
- Do I understand you to be saying _____?

A related follow-up technique involves asking for support and justification for responses. Here are examples:

- Why do you think that?
- What's your evidence?
- What's your reasoning?
- Can you find support in the text/data?
- How do the data support your conclusion?
- But earlier, didn't we say that _____, which seems to be at odds with what you're saying now? Can you clarify?
- How does that square with what the text says on page ___?

The regular request for support makes it clear that answers and opinions are necessary but not sufficient. As with the doctoral dissertation, students must be able to *defend* a position, not just have one.

Devil's Advocate

Another well-established technique for pushing student thinking is for teachers (and eventually students) to assume the role of devil's advocate. By deliberately challenging students' interpretations or conclusions, or presenting an alternative viewpoint, we press for clarification and justification. Here are samples of devil's advocate follow-ups:

- I disagree. Convince me.
- How would you respond to those who say _____?
- Have you considered another perspective?
- Who has a completely different idea or reason?
- Is it really either/or? Might there be different "right" answers or ways of thinking about this?

It is important that you explain this role that you are playing so that learners do not take your stance personally. (One teacher we know puts on Halloween-costume devil's horns to humorously signal a serious point—that she will challenge their thinking!) Over time, we would hope that students would (respectfully) take on a devil's advocate role with each other, especially during debates and Socratic seminars. By extension, we can ask students to argue for the view that is the opposite of the one they believe, a strategy common in training for forensics or debate class.

Handling Inaccurate or Inappropriate Responses

Predictably, some students will respond to classroom questions, including essential questions, with comments that are inaccurate, thoughtless, silly, and off topic. Sometimes kids will simply try to test the teacher or amuse the class with an inappropriate remark. How one handles these responses early in the school year can set the climate for the remaining days. The art of facilitating inquiry is to understand how to listen, dignify student responses, and make it clear that opinions are necessary but not sufficient: the goal is greater understanding—of both the subject at hand and the answers proposed by students.

Of course, willfully hurtful or obscene statements should not be tolerated. A simple stare-down may be enough to make the point; or you might simply say something such as this: "Kelly, I know you know that such a comment is out of bounds." However, when students are honestly trying, sensitivity to "wrong" or impulsive answers is in order. Our advice here is straightforward: respond to student answers in a nonevaluative, depersonalized fashion as much as possible. Avoid put-downs—any comment or tone of voice that will make a student look foolish or feel stupid—particularly when students make errors in factual information or reasoning. In some cases you can help learners clarify their thinking by using the various probes already described. In other cases, you can quickly correct the fact cited but underscore the importance of the question. Alternately, it may be best to redirect the question and involve other learners.

A general rule of thumb is to acknowledge any appropriate, albeit flawed, response as a contribution, and to set the tone that mistakes are a necessary and expected part of learning. Indeed, the common phrase "coming to an understanding" suggests a process over time. Few of us attain deep insight instantaneously, which is why revisiting an essential question over time is . . . essential.

All these tips and response techniques for using essential questions can be reduced to a simple rule of thumb: the teacher's role is to invite thoughtful responses and questions, serve as an unobtrusive referee, and be a careful listener.

Inviting Students' Questions

No doubt you're wondering about the relationship between essential questions developed by teachers and questions generated by students. If student inquiry is the aim, why not allow instruction to be driven by student questions? More generally, then: What is the role of student questions when planning and teaching via essential questions?

A recent book makes the point clearly in its title: *Make Just One Change: Teach Students to Ask Their Own Questions* (Rothstein & Santana, 2011). The authors make an elegant case for the importance of developing student questioning, and they provide a practical framework to accomplish it. Their argument echoes that of John Dewey, made a century earlier; that is, democracy depends upon active participation by citizens, and a most empowering form of participation is to be able to ask the questions, not merely respond to the questions of others.

A related case for student questioning comes from research in reading. Researchers Annemarie Palincsar and Ann Brown found that when readers frame their own questions, they are engaged more actively in processing of text and meaning-making. In addition, students who ask their own questions can check their own comprehension rather than relying only on teacher questions and feedback (Palincsar & Brown, 1984; Raphael, 1986).

Although we fully support the end goal of autonomous and proactive student questioning, we offer a caution. If teachers merely elicit and run with student questions without framing overarching curricular goals and essential questions to support them, then there can be no guaranteed and viable curriculum. In fact, there is little likelihood of students coming up with questions that serve to open doors to deep understanding (as the subtitle of this book suggests) in science, literature, math, art, and other subject areas because often the big ideas are abstract and counterintuitive. Put more bluntly, although children are amazingly curious and inquisitive, some of their questions lead to intellectual dead ends or tangential, though fun, meanderings. (Those of us who went to school or taught in the 1960s and 1970s will likely recall the "go with the flow" looseness of that era, which had its charms but was often insufficiently purposeful or productive.)

As professionals, it is *our* job to know which questions meet the two distinct sides of the coin: questions that both engender student interest and provide the greatest likelihood of depth and success in subject matter understanding. Yes, a great teacher can work with student questions to shape learning to hit academic targets, but putting the issue in the hands of students hides the key idea: teachers must know the key questions and ideas at the heart of what they teach and work tactfully yet firmly toward achieving academic goals while also working to develop interests and talents. This distinction is also as old as Dewey: we must not conflate "what the students are interested in" with learning that is "in the students' interest."

Thus the question "Who should pose the questions?" is a false dichotomy. It is an issue not of teacher questions versus student questions, but of how to blend both in a purposeful manner. The point of essential questions, in other words, is not merely to engender student curiosity, but also to help students inquire into the important ideas of the disciplines at the core of a good education. *Both* goals have to be attained: academic understanding and personal meaning via questions and the disciplined pursuit of them.

That said, effective use of essential questions inevitably leads to an increase in the number of student questions. It must be so. For as we have repeatedly said, the best essential questions need to be questioned, and all proposed answers must be treated as tentative, thus open to critical and imaginative questioning in response. Nor should our caution about overreliance on student questions as the basis for curriculum be understood as a rejection of student-generated projects, problems, or investigations. On the contrary, many of the best curricular units provide students with rich opportunities to explore ideas and issues on their own terms. An education for meaning and the development of autonomy demand such opportunities. We merely call attention to the required blend: teachers and students together use questions to develop needed understanding that is of interest to all as well as in everyone's interest.

Developing Questioning Autonomy

A long-term goal of using essential questions is that students eventually become the askers and pursuers of such questions without being directed by the teacher. How, then, is autonomous questioning best developed?

In the research on literacy, a common phrase used to describe the long-term aim of autonomous reading and comprehension by students is "the gradual release of responsibility" by the teacher. Pearson and Gallagher (1983) coined this phrase to describe how teachers can gradually wean learners away from adult assistance so that they can eventually perform a task independently. Here is a succinct summary of the idea provided by researchers Annemarie Palincsar and Ann Brown (1984):

> Children first experience a particular set of cognitive activities in the presence of experts, and only gradually come to perform these functions by themselves. First, an expert (parent, teacher, master craftsman, etc.) guides the child's activity, doing most of the cognitive work herself. The child participates first as a spectator, then as a novice responsible for very little of the actual work. As the child becomes more experienced and capable of performing more complex aspects of the task, aspects that she has seen modeled by adults time and time again, the adult gradually cedes her greater responsibility. The adult and child come to share the cognitive work, with the child taking initiative and the adult correcting and guiding where she falters. Finally, the adult allows the child to take over the major thinking role and adopts the stance of a supportive and sympathetic audience. Initially, the supportive other acts as the model, critic, and interrogator, leading the child to use more powerful strategies and to apply them more widely. In time, the interrogative, critical role is adopted by the child, who becomes able to fulfill some of these functions for herself via self-regulation and self-interrogation. Mature learners are capable of providing the interrogative critical role for themselves. (p. 123)

Although originally developed for reading instruction, the *gradual release of teacher responsibility* model offers a general schema for the development of independent mastery in *any* subject, at *any* age, in *any* setting in or out of school. Here are two simple protocols for putting the progression from dependency to autonomy into operation:

- I do; you watch.
- I do; you help.
- You do; I help.
- You do; I watch.

- I model it; you do it.
- You do it; I give feedback and guidance.
- You practice and refine; you self-assess.
- You do it; I observe.

Here's a sample rubric for measuring the degree of student autonomy:

Level of Independence	Descriptor
Independent	Learner completes task effectively with complete autonomy.
Lightly scaffolded	Learner completes task with minimal assistance (e.g., 1–2 hints or reminding cues from teacher).
Scaffolded	Learner needs step-by-step instructions and scaffolding tools (e.g., a graphic organizer and a checklist) to complete the task.
Simplified task, with considerable support	Learner needs the task simplified; requires constant feedback and advice, review, and reteaching; needs constant encouragement to complete the task.
No independence	The learner cannot complete the task, even with considerable support.

Progressions of this sort can naturally apply to the use of essential questions. Whether we focus on the teacher (gradual release) or the student (increasing responsibility), the point is the same. Over time students need to become increasingly autonomous in advancing the inquiry and discussion, either by asking questions or by responding to them on their own. Your goal as teacher? Make yourself obsolete over time!

Socratic Seminar

A formal approach for the self-directed involvement of learners in the exploration of essential questions is known as the Socratic seminar. Mortimer Adler popularized this idea 30 years ago in *The Paideia Proposal* (1982), though it has old roots in the Great Books program at St. John's College and the seminar approach used at Columbia University and the University of Chicago. Adler argued for a system of three explicitly different educational goals—acquisition of organized knowledge, development of intellectual skills, and enlarged understanding of ideas and values—supported by three associated forms of pedagogy. According to Adler, the third goal, enlarged understanding,

> is neither didactic nor coaching. It cannot be teaching by telling and by using textbooks. It must be the Socratic mode of teaching because it helps the student bring ideas to birth. It is teaching by asking questions, by leading discussions, by helping students raise their minds up . . . to a state of understanding or appreciating. (p. 29)

The Socratic seminar provides a disciplined structure for using essential questions to explore and uncover important ideas from texts. Elfie Israel (2002) succinctly defines Socratic seminars and their rich benefits for participants:

> The Socratic seminar is a formal discussion, based on a text, in which the leader asks open-ended questions. Within the context of the discussion, students listen closely to the comments of others, thinking critically for themselves, and articulate their own thoughts and their responses to the thoughts of others. They learn to work cooperatively and to question intelligently and civilly. (p. 89)

As these accounts suggest, a seminar aims at *sustained* inquiry and meaning-making by students. The aim is not only attainment of an expert's understanding. The intent is for students to "play the game" of an expert inquirer—that is, to improve at asking and answering important questions, making defensible and systematic interpretations, supported by evidence and logic. Once underway, the aim of the seminar is to probe the points being made, to ensure that we understand what is being said and to balance it against what else has been said and cited as evidence previously. Thus, in a seminar, the essential question is not merely used to engage students in a conversation about content in order to acquire more knowledge. Its more fundamental purpose requires active meaning-making—attempts to frame an understanding and try that understanding out on others. This is the essence of constructivism: meaning is crafted not by teachers but by learners.

As the reference to "playing the game" also suggests, a seminar is more like what student athletes and artists do rather than what happens in a typical teacher-directed class. As on the field or the stage, the aim is for students to be autonomous, proactive, and strategic users of knowledge and skill. As in soccer or basketball, it is contrary to the very point of performance if students passively wait for the coach or teacher to direct every next "move"—whether on the field or in the classroom. Rather, the students must learn to take on teacher moves—asking questions of one another, pointing out inconsistencies in what has been said—and teachers must learn to be quiet and to listen carefully.

In a seminar, the teacher is a coach of student inquiry in another sense. She is a coach who, after brief instruction, retreats to the sideline to observe and listen as students play the game of collaborative and personal inquiry. Before and after the "playing," the teacher, like any coach, offers training in the skills and strategies of collaborative inquiry and discussion and provides specific feedback and needed remediation to the class and to individuals, based on their performance.

In short, the Socratic seminar is *not* a more conversational form of instruction. Rather, a seminar (and more generally the use of essential questions) offers students the opportunity to get better at self-regulated inquiry, with increasing freedom from teacher cues, prompts, and other supports.

Whether one uses a formal structure such as the Socratic seminar or merely signals to students that collaborative inquiry is the goal of an activity or a unit, the implications for teaching should be clear: students need to know—by teacher actions and procedures—that in-depth inquiry is required, not optional.

FAQ

I like the idea of using a Socratic seminar, but I have no experience in this method. Can you recommend some ways of getting started?

A seminar requires five basic things: (1) a common source (a "text" in the broadest meaning of the term), (2) dedicated time and organization of space that support shared inquiry, (3) rules of engagement, (4) clear goals that make clear the point of the seminar and the criteria by which it will be judged (making clear how different it is from typical teacher-led instruction), and (5) a great question that opens the seminar and to which it continually returns.

The most important thing to do in getting started is to pick the basis of the seminar. You need a rich, thought-provoking, somewhat puzzling text, experience, or data along with a question that cannot be answered with a yes or no. In other words, there has to be a real problem or issue worth grappling with. Inquiry cannot begin until there is a source that raises questions that need probing and yields many plausible and diverse answers. That's why seminars have historically been established around "great books" or other rich texts (books, articles, movies, intractable problems).

Common and suitable texts for older students include the *Declaration of Independence,* Martin Luther King's *Letter from Birmingham Jail,* or Plato's *Apology.* For young students, any of the *Frog and Toad Are Friends* stories can be used to explore the question "Who is a true friend?" There are also developed programs—Junior Great Books, Paideia, Touchstones—that offer excellent sources of readings for seminars.

Math and science teachers can either choose an interesting reading on a key topic (such as *Flatland,* by E. A. Abbott, or an essay on the nature of science by Richard Feynman) or pose a problem or an experiment that is designed to raise as many (if not more) questions than it answers. False proofs are always interesting and revealing (e.g., the "proof" that $1 = 0$), as are experiments with counterintuitive findings (light interfering with light equals dark).

Once you have chosen a suitably rich source, make clear the goal and the new rules of the game called "shared inquiry." Point out that as the "coach," you will be mostly on the sideline (though you reserve the right to ask questions or point out interesting problems), as the students are the players. Start small; perhaps hold a seminar once a week, for 20 minutes. Allow time to process the experience: What happened? What worked—and what didn't? How might you improve?

Once students have been introduced to the process, you are now ready to pose an intriguing question that becomes the helpful lens for making meaning of the text. The question might initially be topical. For example, for the book *Catcher in the Rye,* the question might be "What's wrong with Holden?" or you might choose a broader essential question, such as "How well do we know ourselves?"

5

How Do We Address
Implementation Challenges and Special Cases?

Musician John Lennon clearly knew something about education. His famous aphorism "Life is what happens when you're busy making other plans" resonates with every teacher who has seen a beautifully crafted lesson plan go out the window within five minutes of its confrontation with real kids in real classrooms. Working with EQs only increases the likelihood that something might go wrong, because teachers are not only trying out new and demanding approaches but also opening up instruction to a far less predictable set of outcomes as students take more ownership of classroom inquiry and discourse. Smart curriculum designers thus plan to adjust in the likelihood that things won't go as planned. It is wise to anticipate what may go awry in the use of EQs and be prepared to make changes when such unwanted outcomes occur.

In this chapter we consider some of the most common and important challenges that teachers are likely to encounter when working with essential questions and offer some tips on how to troubleshoot those rough spots. We'll also explore special cases of using EQs with young children and in particular subject areas.

The likely difficulties can be grouped under two general headings: (1) ineffective or inappropriate responses (by both teacher and students) to the demands of unscripted discussion, and (2) anxiety in the face of the inherent unpredictability of inquiry and the related fear of losing control (by teachers) or looking foolish (by students). New roles, skills, and norms need to be practiced and learned. As in learning to play a new game or musical instrument, there is a predictable learning curve in which error and frustration are inevitable. That likelihood leads to anxiety, for both teacher and students, because predictability is highly prized yet hard to come by when we are truly learning something new.

How, then, might we get beyond the unavoidable anxiety of in-depth inquiry into EQs? Once everyone is comfortable with collaborative inquiry and its rituals, the richness of discussion and subsequent insights are often self-reinforcing. But initially, teacher fear of giving students power to chart the course of inquiry and discussion, along with student anxiety in the face of no single right or final answer, are powerful psychological hurdles to overcome.

Two thousand years ago, Plato famously depicted our anxiety in the face of genuine inquiry in the allegory of the cave, a "parable of our ignorance and education," as he frames it initially. We are asked to imagine mankind shackled inside a cave and able only to view shadows of held-up objects cast on a wall by the light of a fire:

> At first, when any of them is liberated and compelled suddenly to stand up and turn his neck round and walk and look towards the light, he will suffer sharp pains; the glare will distress him, and he will be unable to see the realities of which in his former state he had seen the shadows.
>
> Now, consider someone saying to him, that what he saw before was an illusion, but that now, when he is approaching nearer to reality and he has a clearer vision—what will be his reply? Will he not assume that the shadows which he formerly saw are truer than the objects which are now shown to him?
>
> Far truer.
>
> And if he is compelled to look straight at the light, will he not have a pain in his eyes which will make him turn away to take refuge in the objects of vision which he can see, and which he will presume to be in reality clearer than the things which are now being shown to him?
>
> True, he said.
>
> And suppose once more, that he is reluctantly dragged up a steep and rugged ascent, and held fast until he is forced into the presence of the sun himself, is he not likely to be pained and irritated? When he approaches the light his eyes will be dazzled, and he will not be able to see anything at all of what are now called realities.

Metaphorically, the parable posits that a true education releases us from our blindness. Yet Plato warns us that there is a paradox in genuine learning. Questioning what we think we know is psychologically difficult, and learners predictably resist it. We prefer the comfort of the known and the expected. So the resistance to the new and uncertain leads to a host of unwitting behaviors that undercut collaborative inquiry—even if everyone, teacher and student, feels more in control as a result.

Here is a similarly vivid, modern-day account from Walter Bateman (1990) about what it may feel like at first for any teacher in this new role of someone who asks questions and gives oneself over to what happens next:

> So you are actually brave enough to try one class of teaching by inquiry. You prepare for the big day. You have a problem ready to start the class. You pose

that problem. You wait for an answer. Three seconds later, you begin to panic. Your hands sweat. The class just stares at you dumbly.

Calm down. Students need time to think. They need time to digest the very notion that you actually want them to think. They need time to figure out what the question meant and also whether they dare stick their necks out.

Wait.

Smile. Don't even glance at your wristwatch. Stare expectantly at one or two students that you normally count on to be ready. Nudge them a little with your smile.

Wait. Don't say a word. Smile expectantly.

Wait.

In two or three hours, someone will offer a tentative response. Should you be able to sneak a glance at the time, you will find that those two hours were really forty seconds.

Glory be, the student who speaks up gives the "correct" response right out of the text. In sheer gratitude you want to shout: "Good for you. That's right. I knew I could count on you."

Don't you dare. Don't you dare tell that student that the answer is right. Don't you dare deny the class the fun of thinking and deciding and judging.

Instead, you turn and lay that delight on some other student. "Do you agree with that?"

Shock. Many students have never been asked that . . .

The students will survive. You will live through it. With a bit of patience and practice, both you and the students will learn to discuss an issue, to question an assumption, to define a word, to explore alternatives, to gain the skills needed for thinking. Since you already know how to do this, your job is to learn to be quiet. (p. 183)

With practice and the experience of seeing how students really can achieve positive results with less teacher direction, as in Plato's allegory, we, too, eventually see clearly and grasp that the new way is superior to the old. Our new role as quiet listener and probing questioner is in fact quite powerful, even more so than merely being a teacher/director. (Indeed, this was the moral of the story explicitly drawn by Socrates for his listeners.)

Yet it takes time to overcome our anxiety and the consequences of that fear. As an example, Grant tells the story of a middle school teacher whom he helped implement the use of the Socratic seminar. First Grant modeled the process, facilitating a seminar with her students for a period. Then the teacher conducted two sessions with Grant observing and giving feedback. The progress in the teacher's skill and apparent comfort was tangible, and Grant noted it. However, the teacher made a curious evaluation of her own performance: she viewed the second episode as far less successful than the first. Yet to an observer, the data suggested the opposite: in the second class, more students spoke overall (all but 2 of 26, versus a third of the students in the first class); the teacher asked far fewer leading, low-level questions; and student-to-student interactions doubled in number compared with the first class. When asked why she made her judgment as she did, her response revealed the challenge in adjusting to a world of less clear outcomes and moves. She felt the second class was more "crazy" and "out of control" than the first, and she felt far less sure of what to say and when to say it. Those feelings blinded her to the positive results the observer's data revealed.

Such dread of loss of control with in-depth inquiry is thus likely no matter how much tolerance for uncertainty a teacher has. We can temporarily lose our bearings about what it means to be a teacher. With older students, especially, we fear chaos breaking out as the "inmates run the asylum." Furthermore, we may have added anxiety about being viewed as a "bad" teacher by supervisors who might judge our teaching by traditional teacher-focused indicators. (Indeed, we have heard of teachers facilitating a Socratic seminar during which a supervisor stops by for a walk-through or class visit, only to have the supervisor leave, saying, "Oh, I'll come back when you are teaching.") Anyone who has taken the leap and persisted in the face of these fears knows the happy ending: students are likely to rise to the occasion if we let them and guide them well. So the challenge for teachers is to find a more comfortable psychological space in which to become increasingly at ease in thinking and acting like a coach—that is, guiding and then gradually releasing control, rather than trying to oversee every move and behavior.

Yet once we find that comfortable space in which we act like a coach, we come face to face with the lesson of the cave all over again: many *students* actively resist open inquiry and discussion. A very bright but clearly agitated student calls out in the middle of a Socratic seminar, "Enough discussion, Mr. Wiggins! Tell us what the reading means!" Similarly, a teacher in a UbD workshop unhappily pleads, "Just give me an essential question! I can't think of any!" These are just two of many manifestations of resistance to in-depth inquiry that we have faced and that readers will predictably encounter. Thus the rough spots in using essential questions involve more than just a lack of skill on the part of teacher and students. We must be prepared to help people become less anxious and more comfortable with the *inherent* uncertainties of inquiry into EQs that, by definition, have no simple answer.

Once we recognize that such fear, not just questioning techniques and performance deficits, plays a role in the success of the class, we can, like a good coach, better assess what moves help reduce the fear of failure and uncertainty. So, be proactive. Self-assess your own comfort level by considering the following reflective questions:

- What kinds of and how many questions do I ask?
- Do students understand this new "game" and its "rules"? Are students acting as if they understand the goal, roles, and moves of effective collaborative inquiry?
- Am I calmly and patiently putting the onus on students, as if to say "You can do it; I'm here to help"?
- Am I projecting fear or confidence as a coach? Regardless of what I feel inside, am I exuding a warm and confident attitude? (Note that in the Bateman story the teacher smiles at students he seeks to engage.)
- Is there enough silence (wait time) for thoughts and responses to form? Am I showing a comfort with silence?
- Am I unwittingly undercutting inquiry and discussion (e.g., by calling only on volunteers or never questioning or challenging student responses)?
- If student contributions are not ideal, which of my responses involve more people in the discussion and enhance the ideas offered, and which may stifle the inquiry?
- Do my assignments and assessments make clear that questions and thoughtful pursuit of them really matter, or is it possible to get *A*s in my class by remaining passive and merely learning the content?

None of us is a perfect teacher; most of us will not have ideal answers to these questions. Indeed, these are timeless essential questions for all educators! However, the more we dispassionately and deliberately attend to the gap between our goal and the inevitable rough spots, and take steps to shape the classroom accordingly, the more likely we are to be successful.

With these general considerations in mind, we direct you to Figure 5.1, which charts a summary of challenging issues for teachers and learners in the use of EQs, followed by suggested actions. Clearly, these concerns and brief troubleshooting suggestions are just a start. Readers are encouraged to explore some of the suggested articles and books on questioning (listed in the Annotated Bibliography in Appendix A) to better understand potential difficulties and solutions to them.

We now turn our attention to some special challenging cases in the use of essential questions.

Making Essential Questions Kid-Friendly

When educators (especially of younger children) begin to craft essential questions, they often ask, "Should the essential question be framed in 'kid language' or stated in the way in which adults think about it?" Our slightly cheeky response is yes. We should do both!

Figure 5.1 Implementation Issues, Indicators, and Troubleshooting Suggestions

Issue: Unclear on the goal of collaborative inquiry

Teacher-related indicators

Teacher acts and speaks as if the meaning of the question, the nature of dialogue, and the value of inquiry should seem obvious to learners.

- Believes that just posting or asking the question is sufficient for students to run with the process.
- Becomes frustrated when students do not respond or offer superficial answers.
- Is disappointed by lack of support for answers or for varied points of view.

Student-related indicators

Students think that there is one "best" answer or that any response to an open question is OK.

- Answers are spontaneous and glib.
- Speaker feels no need to clarify or support what was said.
- Answers are often off topic, unfocused, or random.
- Students are puzzled by request to justify their contribution.
- Students seek teacher's help ("Just tell us what you want").

Suggestions

- Review the purpose, rules, and protocols for inquiry and discussions of EQs.
- Remind students that quality, not quantity, of participation is what is desired.
- Make clear that two or three different answers may all offer valid interpretations.
- Highlight and praise, if necessary, answers that build on and connect to proposed ideas by others.
- Identify possible weaknesses or unexamined assumptions in answers that students are too quick to accept.
- Preface next discussion with reminders about the traits of an effective response.

Issue: Fear

Teacher-related indicators

Teacher is fearful of a loss of control and a loss of respect as "authority."

- Teacher overly directs the discussion (it seems more like a recitation model).
- Only calls on the most able students.
- Is visibly concerned by or unhappy with tentative or off-target student answers.
- Appears visibly nervous or ill at ease.

Student-related indicators

Students are fearful of standing out and looking foolish.

- Some students will look down or away to avoid being called on.
- Facial expressions and nervous laughter indicate fear and anxiety.
- A student is silent in class but talkative about the topic before and after class.
- A student prefaces a comment with "I know this sounds really stupid, but . . ."

Suggestions

- Think like a coach; watch the students "play the game" and take notes for later follow-up.
- Provide think time and ask learners to write some notes about what they will contribute when/if called upon.
- Share ideas in groups of two or three first; then come up with a single contribution.
- Alert shy or quiet students to a question that you will ask to enable them to prepare.
- Teacher (and students) might watch a video of a model discussion to better understand the nature of the activity, how it works, and how a different kind of control is required.

Figure 5.1 *(continued)*

Issue: Discomfort with silence and ambiguity

Teacher-related indicators
Teacher is visibly uncomfortable with silence and ambiguity.

- Does not provide wait time.
- Looks and acts pained by silence.
- Keeps trying to answer student questions and judging student answers.
- Suggests that there is an unambiguous answer to the EQ if students would only hunt for it.

Student-related indicators
Students are visibly uncomfortable with silence and ambiguity.

- They look at the teacher for next move.
- They fidget and look uneasy when there is silence.
- Students plead, "Just tell us, OK?"
- Students seek teacher confirmation after a contribution (e.g., "Is that right?").
- Students ask the teacher to answer the question.

Suggestions
- Do a think-aloud and feel-aloud to model the unease that anyone of any age may experience in a discussion of an open-ended question.
- Ask students to describe in writing what they feel before and during class discussions. Discuss their responses and look for patterns.
- Provide and discuss brief readings on stage fright or discomfort with ambiguity.
- Remind students of protocols/rules/rubrics that stress the importance of engaging and taking a risk.

Issue: Overly focused on content

Teacher-related indicators
Teacher is concerned about content coverage.

- Treats the EQ as simply a rhetorical device or a hook for setting up direct instruction on a topic.
- Cuts off discussion just as it is about to get going (e.g., "We have to move on . . .").

Student-related indicators
Students are overly focused on content acquisition and assessments.

- Student is worried about what is graded and tested by the teacher (e.g., "Will this count?").
- Student constantly seeks teacher help (e.g., "Just tell us what we need to know, please").

Suggestions
- Make clear that the goal is generalizing from information and differing points of view, not merely finding facts.
- Make clear the difference between facts and opinions, data and inferences based on data.

Issue: EQs and answers too convergent and narrow in scope

Teacher-related indicators
Teacher questions and comments are leading.

- The question has only one best answer.
- Teacher seems too eager to get to a preferred answer.
- Teacher asks lots of "what" and "when" and "how did" questions.
- "Why" questions point toward a factual answer that can be looked up.

Continued on next page

Figure 5.1 *(continued)*

Student-related indicators

Students try to state, guess, or find the "right" answer rather than thinking deeply.

- Students make comments and use a tone of voice suggesting that their contribution should end the matter.
- Once an answer is given, most students stop thinking.

Suggestions
- Ask more "why" and "what if" questions.
- Even when someone gives a really good answer, ask, "Is there another way to look at this? Are there other possible answers?"
- Ask students to respond to the prompt "I used to think . . . Now I think . . ."

Issue: EQs and answers too divergent and broad in scope

Teacher-related indicators

Teacher questions are vague, ambiguous, or unfocused; too broad to bring satisfactory closure.

- "What's the idea here?"
- "What do the data mean?"

Student-related indicators

Students don't seem to see the purpose of the question or know how to respond.

- Students avert eyes and look uncomfortable.
- Facial expressions indicate students are puzzled.
- Students ask, "What are you asking?"
- Students struggle for words (though they are trying to participate).

Suggestions
- Rephrase or reframe the question in simpler terms.
- Emphasize a more concrete manifestation of the question. For example, if "What is good writing?" doesn't generate any useful responses, ask, "What's the difference between a good read and a great book?"

Issue: Too aggressive

Teacher-related indicators

Teacher questioning and probing are overly aggressive and intimidating to students.

- "Why on earth would you say *that*?"
- "How can you possibly think . . . ?"
- "What would make you offer such a statement?"

Student-related indicators

Students are posturing and striving to "win" or be "correct."

- "That makes no sense."
- "Prove it!"
- "Let me tell you the right answer and what's wrong with yours."

Suggestions
- Model appropriate versus inappropriate behavior in response to a less than ideal comment.
- Jokingly remind students of the penalty box in hockey or the foul call in basketball. List and talk about "foul" moves in discussion. View and listen to examples from talk TV and radio.
- Remind people of the code of conduct and how discussion differs from debate.
- Assign group grades for the discussion, not just an individual grade.
- Apologize if you said something that was clearly inappropriate.

Figure 5.1 *(continued)*

Issue: Too nice

Teacher-related indicators
Teacher doesn't probe and critique student contributions.

- "Interesting idea, Kate."
- "Thanks for sharing, Joe."
- "Good" (without qualifying why it is good).

Student-related indicators
Students seem unwilling to disagree with peers or the teacher.

- Students remain silent in the face of a clearly incorrect, problematic, controversial, or unusual comment.
- Students become insecure, angry, or embarrassed if their contributions are challenged in any way.

Suggestions
- Make clear that questioning an answer need not be threatening or aggressive.
- Use follow-ups, like "Do I understand you to be saying . . . ?" "Where is that interesting idea supported by the text?" "I'm not following you; can you explain your thinking (idea or argument)?"
- Make a point of playing devil's advocate (perhaps with a plastic pitchfork available as a prompt to break the ice).
- Play dumb; for example, "I am not getting what you are saying, Joe. Help me understand your reasoning." "Boy, I must be dense. I don't see that in the text. Can you help me out?"

Issue: Too little difference of opinion

Teacher-related indicators
There is no variety in responses.

- Does not encourage students to consider the EQ from a different point of view.

Student-related indicators
Students do not offer a variety of responses to the EQ.

- Students may not have read the text or completed the task.
- Students may take a literal approach and be looking and listening for the "right" answer.
- Student comments suggest that if something is in a book, it must be true; they believe that issues are black or white; they are uncomfortable with shades of gray.

Suggestions
- Bring in book reviews, op-ed pieces, or conflicting articles to show that intelligent and informed people can disagree on important questions.
- Play devil's advocate.
- Set up a formal debate, and explain why you are doing it.

Issue: Domination

Teacher-related indicators
Teacher talks too much.

- Answers the question for students.
- Responds after every comment, offering own opinion.

Student-related indicators
One or more students talk too much, while others become more silent and passive.
- Some students are oblivious or ignore the fact that they dominate.
- Some students make sweeping, confident-sounding generalizations.

Continued on next page

Figure 5.1 *(continued)*

Suggestions
- Ask the dominant students to take a few minutes of time-out during which they take notes or become a process observer to code the conversation in terms of who said what and the nature of the contribution.
- Divide the class into two groups, putting the students who tend to dominate in one group, then asking that group to be observers and note-takers while the other group discusses; then switch roles.
- Remind students that it is in their interest to get as many possible views on the table as possible to ensure that all perspectives and ideas are to be considered.

Issue: Insensitive, rude, immature comments, and tone of voice

Teacher-related indicators
Teacher puts down a person or a contribution.

- Is sarcastic.
- Rolls eyes when someone speaks.
- Makes insulting comment about a student or the student's contribution.

Student-related indicators
Students are sarcastic, or they put down a person or legitimate contribution.

Suggestions
- If the teacher says something rude, the teacher should immediately apologize and remind people of the rules of discourse. Or the teacher can make it a teachable moment: "What did I just do, and how was it not helpful to the process?"
- If students say rude things or behave inconsiderately, try to enlist the class as a whole in recognizing and policing such behavior, even if in the short term you have to gently but firmly call such behavior out of bounds.
- Try to find a student whose body language suggests disdain toward or impatience with such student rudeness, and ask, "You made a face. Would you please explain why?"

Keep in mind the difference between planning and teaching. When we first begin to *plan* a unit, we consider the overall goals—standards, understandings, knowledge, and skills. It is in this context that essential questions are typically selected or generated. At this point it is important for the teacher to be clear on just what questions really matter in teaching for understanding. Ultimately, however, the *audience* for the essential question is the learner. We want to entice students' thinking by casting the question in a way that is relevant and accessible to them. Hence, there is often a need to edit, modify, or adapt an "adult" version of a question to make it kid-friendly. Here are three examples of such modifications:

• A middle school English/language arts teacher developed the following essential question to guide students' reading, discussion, and writing: "How does a peer group influence the beliefs and actions of early adolescents?" The question was appropriate for the short stories and novels that made up part of her syllabus, and certainly the question is relevant to the age group. However, the teacher found that the question never resonated with her students, because they viewed it as too "preachy." Based on the suggestions of her students, she revised the question to this: "Why do some people sometimes act stupid when they are in groups?" It proved to be a winner—instantly engaging while holding student interest over the long term and keyed to the literature under consideration.

• A teacher used the following question in a unit on Russian history within a global studies course: "Was Gorbachev a hero or a traitor to his country?" The question focused learning activities and the culminating debate in which the students role-played various Russian leaders (Gorbachev, Yeltsin, Lenin, Stalin, Marx, Trotsky, and Catherine the Great) in a "meeting of the minds" format. Then they had writing options (e.g., a mock newspaper article, an editorial, or an essay) for responding to the EQ. After using the question with several classes, the teacher realized that it could be both punchier and broader, so he changed it to "Who blew it?"

• An elementary teacher adapted her original adult-language EQ, "How do geography, climate, and natural resources of a region impact the economy and lifestyle of people in that region?" to "How does *where* we live influence *how* we live?"

Just as "the proof of the pudding is in the eating," the value of an essential question is revealed in use; that is, can students relate to it? Does it stimulate thinking and discussion? Will its exploration lead to deepening understanding? If not, then editing is in order.

Essential Questions in Mathematics

As previously noted, we have found that teachers of mathematics at all levels often struggle in formulating and using essential questions. We attribute this pattern in large part to the ways in which grade-level math standards are typically written (as lists of discrete concepts and skills); the ways they are packaged in textbooks; the ways they are assessed (via decontextualized items with correct answers); and the formulaic ways of teaching rules and algorithms (e.g., "Yours is not to reason why; just invert and multiply"). Such framing of math content does not naturally lend itself to a classroom centered on essential questions.

One recommendation in Chapter 3 was to employ a set of overarching EQs that spiral across the grades, focusing on the big ideas and key processes of mathematics (e.g., "How can mathematics be used to measure, model, and calculate change?"). Then, appropriate EQs from this set can be applied to *particular* skills and topics (e.g., "How can we measure, model, and calculate change using fractions?").

Another viable approach for using EQs in mathematics is suggested by the Common Core State Standards (CCSS). In addition to traditional content standards, the developers of the CCSS have identified a set of practice standards that characterize desirable thinking processes and habits of mind. These lend themselves to naturally recurring EQs that can be applied across topics and levels. Here are the eight practice standards with corresponding essential questions:

1. **Make sense of problems and persevere in solving them.** What kind of a problem is this? What must be found? What is known? What is unknown? What counts as an adequate solution? Does my answer make sense? Does my approach make sense? What should I do if I'm stuck solving it? What similar problems does this remind me of? What simpler or special cases can help me?

2. **Reason abstractly and quantitatively.** What's the abstract relationship between these specific quantities? What does this quantitative relationship mean? How can I decontextualize the numbers to find a mathematical relationship? Have I represented the relationships between the quantities appropriately? Which operations and equivalences will simplify and help me solve the problem? Does my abstract representation of these quantities make sense in context?

3. **Construct viable arguments and critique the reasoning of others.** Has this been proven? What is assumed? On what assumptions does that inference depend? Where might this assumption logically lead? Is the conclusion logical? Is the conclusion plausible? Have I sufficiently supported my answer and shown my work? Which of these solutions is more plausible? Does this argument make sense? What might be counterevidence and counterarguments to what I have concluded?

4. **Model with mathematics.** What mathematics applies to this situation and these data? What simplifications or approximations should I make in order to make a mathematical model of this phenomena/data/experience? How might the model be refined to be less simplistic and crude? Does this model make sense in this context? How might I test this model? What are the limits of this (or any) mathematical model? How might this model be improved?

5. **Use appropriate tools strategically.** What tools should I use here to be most efficient and effective? What are the strengths and weaknesses of the tools at hand, and might there be better ones for the task? Where might I find more helpful resources when needed?

6. **Attend to precision.** What is the appropriate degree of precision for these particular data and this solution? Have I made my data, reasoning, and conclusion sufficiently clear (for this audience and purpose)? What terms need to be clearly defined? Have I tested the accuracy of my answer? How sure am I? How much statistical confidence should we have in the answer?

7. **Look for and make use of structure.** What's the underlying pattern here? What's the whole, if that's a part? What are the parts, if that's the whole? What type of problem is this? What equivalences or reconstitutions of the problem are likely to help me see a pattern or structure? What shift of perspective might make the solution path more evident?

8. **Look for and express regularity in repeated reasoning.** What regularities suggest a constant relationship at work? What is a summary or shorthand way

of expressing these recurring patterns? What patterns are evident? Am I sure that the general pattern recurs, or is my sample too small? Is that a reasonable way to describe the perceived patterns?

Note: Many of the questions listed under each heading refer explicitly to language and examples used in the narrative explanation of each of the practice standards.

Essential Questions in World Languages

Teachers of modern and classical languages other than English often struggle to develop and fruitfully use essential questions, especially for beginning levels. This is understandable because much of their early instruction focuses on the basic structures of grammar and vocabulary development. Moreover, language teaching and learning (be it English/language arts or world languages) center on procedural knowledge through a spiraling of skills in listening, speaking, reading, and writing. The "content" (declarative knowledge) typically involves literature and culture. Although it is generally easy and comfortable for teachers to develop essential questions for literary themes (such as "heroes") and cultural topics (such as "celebrations"), the skill areas of language prove trickier. Indeed, we often hear language teachers comment that "UbD does not work in our area" since they tend to struggle with Stage 1 (as do teachers in other skill areas, such as music and physical education); this stage, Identify Desired Results, includes determining what essential questions will be considered in a unit.

Given the spiraling nature of language development, we recommend the use of broader, overarching EQs that work across units when teaching the skills of language. We do not mean to suggest that there is no place for unit- or topic-specific questions in language teaching. Indeed, we would expect to see such questions tied to unit themes (e.g., foods) and specific strategies (e.g., summarizing).

Here are some examples of more general EQs that have been fruitfully employed by teachers of languages:

Motivation
- Why learn another language?
- What are my motivations to learn another language?
- What are my expectations about learning another language?
- How will learning a language enhance my life?
- How might learning a language open doors of opportunity?

Learning Process
- What language-learning skills do I already have? How can I use my existing communication skills to learn a new language?
- What are "language patterns," and how can they help me learn and use a new language?

- What are different language-learning styles? How do I determine the most effective language-learning style for me?
  - How can I sound more like a native speaker?
  - What do I do when I am stuck?
  - What can I do to help improve my fluency and accuracy?

Communication

- Why isn't a dictionary enough? Why don't I have to translate everything?
- How do native speakers differ from fluent foreigners?
- In what ways do languages convey meaning?
- How can you "speak" without words? What is "body language"?
- How does language change depending on the situation? Why are different words, expressions, and so on, used with different people? In different situations?
- What do I do when my ideas are more sophisticated than my ability to communicate them?
- How do I keep a conversation going?
- What are the benefits of taking a chance in language? The risks? What mistakes are worth making?
- How is written language different from spoken language? How is spoken language different from written language? How is listening different from reading?

Essential Questions in the Performing Arts

Not surprisingly, teachers of the performing arts often experience similar challenges to those described in earlier sections, especially when their instruction focuses on skill development and practice. As with the teaching of world languages and early literacy, it is tempting to believe that all we have to worry about is building the skill foundation. But this is a disservice to budding musicians, actors, filmmakers, and dancers. At a young age, they need to be asking basic essential questions, such as these: *Did the performance work? What was the tone, vibe, or feeling of that particular performance? How alive was the performance? Was the audience moved? Did we communicate something or convey a feeling?*

Consider the legendary jazz band leader Duke Ellington and his famous song title "It Don't Mean a Thing If It Ain't Got That Swing." That *swing* comes from putting your soul into your work, and that song title arguably applies in a general way to all the performing arts; that is, playing the notes correctly, painting realistically, and reciting the lines accurately are not the ultimate goals. Indeed, in musical circles the term *virtuoso* is sometimes used disparagingly as a subtle put-down, suggesting that although the musician in question may possess great technical skills, he has no soul.

In the performing arts, the deep questions and debates are more likely to deal with the creative process and interpretation, not the skills. For example, try asking students to listen to or watch three different performances of the same song, scene, or dance. How are they the same? How do they differ? What do the performers and directors seem to be trying to communicate by their particular approach? (Here is a simple example in music: ask students to listen to and compare the Martha and the Vandellas version of *Heat Wave* and Linda Ronstadt's version. Emotionally, they are completely different performances and supporting arrangements.)

Accordingly, we encourage visual and performing arts teachers to consider other conceptual strands—Artistic and Creative Process, Interpretation and Critique, and the Role of the Arts in Society—as fruitful arenas for EQs. Here are samples:

Artistic and Creative Process

- Who is an artist? Can anyone be an artist?
- Why do people make art?
- Where do artists get their ideas?
- How is feeling or mood conveyed musically? Visually? Through movement?
- In what way does each art form communicate uniquely?
- What kind of artist am I? What kind of artist could I become?
- How do I use other artists' work to contribute to my own growth?
- How and why does my artwork change?
- To what extent does my artwork change me?
- How do I become accomplished in an art form?

Interpretation and Critique

- How can we "read" and understand a work of art?
- Who determines the meaning of art?
- Does art have a message?
- Should art have a message?
- Is one picture worth a thousand words?
- What makes "great" art?
- Do I like this (music, painting, dance, play)?
- Is the medium the message?
- Are some media better than others for communicating particular ideas or emotions?

The Role of the Arts in Society

- What can works of art tell us about a society?
- How do the arts reflect the time, place, and ideas?
- How do the arts reflect as well as shape culture?
- Do artists have a responsibility to their audiences? To society?
- Should we ever censor artistic expression?
- In what ways have technological changes influenced artistic expression?
- How do artists from different eras explore and express similar themes?

Staying the Course

We know that a brief chapter can only scratch the surface of implementation rough spots and that a book is not the ideal resource for interactive help with troubleshooting issues. And as with any new learning and complex performance, skill takes time, setbacks are predictable, and doubts will creep in. We hope, however, that the frameworks and tips we have provided will give you just enough courage and direction to move forward and to avoid giving up on inquiry-based instruction. You will also find that if you develop a small group or team of people devoted to exploring these approaches together, then two heads are better than one, and just about any difficulty you run into will be solvable by a like-minded group of colleagues and action researchers.

As in Plato's cave allegory, the struggle and resistance are unavoidable. In the end, however, no one happily returns to old habits after seeing the power of unleashing student inquisitiveness.

FAQ

You said that an essential question is open-ended and always provisional. But then it seems like there can't be any essential questions in mathematics, world language, or other skill-focused areas, since the learner just has to simply learn factual material (e.g., vocabulary) and practice key skills.

Look back at the examples of essential questions we gave in math and world language on pages 2 and 3 of Chapter 1, and consider what these questions have in common. They are primarily about issues of strategy, not skill; about metacognition, not facts; about the relative merits of approaches to learning and using skills, not the skills themselves. Mathematicians have argued for hundreds of years over methods of proof; over the meaning and value of such "weird" ideas as irrational, negative, and imaginary numbers; and over the strengths and limits of different mathematical models. Similarly, it is not at all obvious how to most efficiently learn a language or the extent to which cultural understanding affects language learning. We can generalize: in skill areas, essential questions usually focus on issues of *strategic use* of skills rather than the specific skills themselves.

6

How Do We Establish a Culture of Inquiry in Classrooms?

In this book, we have described the qualities of essential questions (*what*), their purpose (*why*), and ways to design and apply them (*how*). But fully realizing the power of essential questions requires a concerted and systematic effort to shape conduct and attitudes to support a culture of inquiry. We alluded to the importance of culture in the previous chapters. Here we take a more comprehensive and detailed look at the elements of culture that have to be shaped, and how.

Nearly a century ago, John Dewey made a prescient observation about classroom culture and questioning that still holds true today:

> No one has ever explained why children are so full of questions outside of the school (so that they pester grown-up persons if they get any encouragement), and the conspicuous absence of display of curiosity about the subject matter of school lessons. Reflection on this striking contrast will throw light upon the question of how far customary school conditions supply a context of experience in which [questions] naturally suggest themselves. (Boydston, 2008, p. 162)

We accept Dewey's premise that learners are far more inquisitive than is suggested by their behaviors in typical classrooms. No doubt you, too, have observed that students' curiosity about academic matters seems to be inversely correlated with their years in school! What accounts for these patterns? What factors discourage classroom inquiry? It is easy to blame society at large. Arguably, factors beyond the school affect student motivation and conduct. Insipid television shows and video games, for example, seem to conspire against thoughtfulness; and political discourse is more about insults than inquiry. Yet, as Dewey's comment highlights, the real issue is the culture of school. Many of the classroom norms we cited in the previous chapter imply that we can and must push beyond fatalistic thinking about wider-world elements beyond our control and look squarely at what *is* improvable in our setting. While not minimizing the challenges of teaching in trying circumstances, we cannot condone a "blame the students, blame the parents, blame society" response. We teach the students we have, and we have a large measure of control over what we do with our time with them.

In his extraordinary synthesis of more than 800 meta-analyses of achievement studies, John Hattie (2009) concluded that there are more than 30 interventions—including high-level questioning, attention to metacognition, and targeted feedback—that have a greater effect on student achievement than socioeconomic status. In fact, there are simply too many counterexamples—teachers in "low-performing" schools who have had extraordinary results with Socratic seminars and project-based learning—to dismiss the possibilities. In one seminar model class we observed in a Louisiana high school, the immediate and unfortunate comment blurted out by the principal was telling: "My, I had no idea our kids could really think!" Similarly, we have been in advanced classes in "good" schools that were as dull as dishwater. Perhaps, then, we have failed to work on those aspects of school culture within our control.

Indeed, we think the famous line from the cartoon character Pogo is at the heart of what inhibits a culture of inquiry: "We have met the enemy and he is us." More than we might wish to acknowledge sometimes, many common classroom routines and teacher actions *do* undercut a culture of questioning. If content coverage and extended teacher talk are the norm, where is the invitation to question? If our assessments primarily reward recall and recognition of facts, where is the opportunity or incentive to think hard about things? If a student is meant to feel stupid after offering an opinion, how likely is it that others will volunteer?

Like the starting point in Alcoholics Anonymous (that is, the first step is to admit there *is* a problem), we contend that the beginning point in establishing a culture of inquiry should involve a staff inquiry into the unintended effects of conventional pedagogy—how it can stifle curiosity, participation, and higher-order thinking. Making deliberate alterations to curriculum, instruction, and classroom routines can have a profound influence on the quality of student engagement and thinking, as both research and common sense confirm.

In this chapter, we explore eight elements within our control that underlie and support a classroom culture of inquiry.

Element #1: Nature of the Learning Goals

To what extent do our teaching practices align with our goals? If understanding and critical thinking are among the desired outcomes, do our curriculum and our assessments reflect these goals? In other words, are we practicing what we preach?

We place alignment of espoused aims with actual practices first because the extent to which the goal of inquiry is put into operation, is transparent, and is given an obvious priority will shape student behaviors and attitudes.

Form must follow function, in the classic architectural maxim. In education, this means that the work we ask students to do and the norms we put in place must align with our learning goals. In the broadest sense, we are referring to curriculum-instruction-assessment (CIA) alignment. As the earlier questions suggest (e.g., why would there be inquiry if the real goal is coverage?), the CIA experience subtly but powerfully shapes the roles and conduct of teachers and students. That explains why well-intentioned teachers, using many of the fine strategies we mentioned in the previous chapters, may find to their dismay that their students don't think as deeply or talk as freely as they expect and desire. It explains why even teachers committed to inquiry can talk too much and elicit too few student responses. But why should this surprise, really? If the curriculum is written in a way that induces lots of teacher coverage of content, and if our tests seek to assess only content mastery, what could send a clearer message to students—in spite of teacher wishes—that in-depth inquiry is at best optional and at worst a *distraction* from efficient coverage?

So if teachers and students alike act on the assumption that acquisition of expert information and skill is the (only) goal, then discussions will be superficial, and the questions will be primarily factual or technical, *regardless* of what teachers and students might sometimes wish for. In a world of coverage, the purpose of a question is to seek information and check recall. We would expect—and we typically find—that most questions are low-level convergent knowledge and comprehension questions, whether asked by students, teachers, or textbooks: *What is . . . ? What are the steps of . . . ? Who was . . . ? When did . . . occur? What is the homework? How do you . . . ? What do we need to know for the quiz? How long does it have to be?* More open questions and lengthy discussions, rather than being welcomed, can thus be seen as tangents or hindrances to coverage!

On the other hand, if classroom assignments, routines, and assessments make clear that in-depth thinking is *required* for success, then we would expect to hear different questions—higher-order divergent questions, such as these: *"Why is . . . ? How might we . . . ? Who has a different idea? But how do you square that claim with her earlier claim that . . . ? What are you assuming when you say . . . ?* Most important, students would know that thoughtful responses to such questions are required for success, and that classroom and homework tasks are designed to elicit them.

This is the primary reason why in the latest version of the Understanding by Design template (what we call "version 2.0"), we now distinguish explicitly between *acquisition* goals, *meaning-making* goals, and *transfer* goals—because these three different goals demand different attention in CIA. Transfer and meaning-making especially require extended student thought and discussion, and our teaching must stimulate and elicit it—by design. Figure 6.1 summarizes some of the more obvious

Figure 6.1 Three Learning Goals and Associated Teaching Roles and Strategies

Learning Goal	Teaching Role and Strategies
Acquisition This goal seeks to help learners *acquire* factual information and basic skills.	**Direct Instruction** In this role, the teacher's primary responsibility is to inform the learners through explicit instruction in targeted knowledge and skills, differentiating as needed. Strategies include: • Diagnostic assessment • Lecture • Advance organizers • Graphic organizers • Questioning (convergent) • Demonstration/modeling • Process guides • Guided practice • Feedback, corrections
Meaning-Making This goal seeks to help learners *construct meaning (that is, come to an understanding)* of important ideas and processes.	**Facilitative Teaching** Teachers in this role engage the learners in actively processing information and guide their inquiry into complex problems, texts, projects, cases, or simulations, differentiating as needed. Strategies include: • Analogies • Graphic organizers • Questioning (divergent) and probing • Concept attainment • Inquiry-oriented approaches • Problem-based learning • Socratic seminar • Reciprocal teaching • Formative (ongoing) assessments • Rethinking and reflection prompts
Transfer This goal seeks to support learners' ability to *transfer* their learning autonomously and effectively in new situations.	**Coaching** In this role, teachers establish clear performance goals, supervise ongoing opportunities to perform (independent practice) in increasingly complex situations, provide models, and give ongoing feedback (as personalized as possible). They also provide "just in time teaching" (direct instruction) when needed. Strategies include: • Ongoing assessment, providing specific feedback in the context of performance • Conferencing • Prompting self-assessment and reflection

distinctions among these three goals and the requisite instructional moves. (For consideration of curriculum reform in the context of Understanding by Design, see Wiggins & McTighe, 2007.)

Here is our maxim about establishing a culture for productive inquiry: walk the talk. If you want thinking and inquiry, you have to ensure that they are required, not optional, vis-à-vis activities, assignments, and assessments. Merely stating and restating the EQs, merely posting questions around the room, simply extending teacher wait time—these efforts by themselves will do little to advance the goal and culture of inquiry. Furthermore, because we are wise to presume that students believe that school learning is simply content acquisition and testing, it will be critical to establish *explicit* time for inquiry into vital questions. Everyone will need to know when it is time to think and share, how such thinking and talk differ from other kinds of classroom thought and talk, and that thoughtful discussions are key goals, not just pleasant tangents.

Mortimer Adler, author of the *Paideia Proposal* (1982) and a fervent advocate for Socratic questioning, strongly advised that special class periods or entire days—the "Wednesday Revolution"—be set up deliberately for nondidactic forms of instruction so as to make crystal-clear to learners that both goal and means are shifting from an acquisition focus to a shared-inquiry and discussion focus. Consider how science labs, art classes, and college seminars do something similar. This kind of control of goals, time, and behaviors is critical for success with essential questions. Otherwise both teacher and students will treat questions as merely rhetorical devices for learning content and miss the power of meaning-making.

Here are several tips for making learning goals explicit and clear—and for making clear when there is a shift in goals from acquisition of content to meaning-making in support of a culture of inquiry:

• Post essential questions prominently around the room, and refer to them regularly (not just at the start of a unit). Make it clear that exploration of these questions is central to the class's study of a given topic or skill area.

• Write out your learning goals for the year in a syllabus, making clear that there are different types of goals that require different kinds of behavior.

• Plan units of study in the UbD Template (version 2.0), in which goals are separated into three kinds: transfer, meaning, acquisition. Code your lessons accordingly, in terms of the goals being addressed in each lesson or activity. (You can read more on this in Modules B and E in *The Understanding by Design Guide to Creating High-Quality Units* [Wiggins & McTighe, 2011].)

• In addition to posting EQs, place a large poster on the wall that highlights the different types of learning goals in your class (e.g., "learn the content," "inquire into essential questions," "apply your learning to challenges and problems," "think critically"), and note verbally and visually when you are shifting the focus from one kind of goal to another. Once the different goals are clear to students via models and instruction, ask them to remind one another what shifts in behavior these different goals demand.

• Select or develop rubrics with attendance to the quality of answers to questions as well as for student questions. Without necessarily grading their contributions, make sure that individual students and the class as a whole understand that active participation and respectful, yet thoughtful, responses are expected from all. Use the rubrics to give feedback to students on the strengths and weaknesses of their responses to EQs. The same rubrics can be used for peer feedback and student self-assessments.

Element #2: The Role of Questions, Teachers, and Students

Having established that inquiry is a vital and different goal from content acquisition, the roles of all participants need to be clarified. From a cultural perspective, three interesting shifts of role occur when working with essential questions: (1) the question has to become more important than any answer; (2) the teacher must become a facilitator and co-inquirer; and (3) students must become their own teachers, increasingly responsible for their own progress. Because these roles may be foreign or puzzling, explicit resources and instruction will be needed for them.

The Role of the Question

The whole idea of essential questions is to signal that the question, not the answer, is what matters. That's why essential *questions,* not essential *answers,* are placed in Stage 1 of UbD—the desired result is deep and sustained questioning, not a particular response.

Almost 50 years ago Jerome Bruner (1965) offered an illuminating explanation for the role of the question in an education designed for in-depth understanding. An organizing question "serves two functions, one of them obvious: putting perspective back into the particulars. The second is less obvious and more surprising. The questions often seemed to serve as criteria for determining where [students] were going and how well they were understanding" (p. 1012). We agree! The question serves as the touchstone; the question becomes the agenda; the question addressed well *is,* in a very real sense, the goal—and so we must get better and better at questioning and returning to essential questions.

Perhaps the best way to make this shift clear is to point to a key feature of *essential* versus *factual* questions. The answers to any essential question are always tentative and often need to be themselves questioned. The role of the answer is thus profoundly different when inquiry is the goal. If a proper inquiry question has been asked, no answer could possibly be final enough to end exploration and discussion, no matter how impressive it sounds. The ideal response to answers, therefore, should be to call for *further* answers and *further* questioning of all the answers. We question an answer to first make sure we understand it, then to better understand why the person proposed it, and (especially) to probe for evidence and reasoning that support it.

So an essential question by its nature leads to *further* questions. In a very real sense, then, *the question is the teacher,* just as in team sports *the game is the teacher* (you may want to post the first of those two statements on the wall next to any posted EQs). Until and unless the essential question is seen as the "teacher," a culture of inquiry is not yet established. In other words, in an inquiry-based environment, an answer is a hypothesis to be tested, not a fact about which no more need be said. That's why—whether in a Socratic seminar, a science lab, or the music studio—the only real arbiter of answers is not the teacher but the effects of pursuing the question in varied ways.

The Role of the Teacher

As a result, our role as the adult in the classroom shifts from that of "answerer" to "facilitator of inquiry," in which we do two things: (1) model and reinforce norms of productive discourse and (2) become careful listeners. A facilitator has four challenges in this role: to almost never answer questions; to almost never evaluate an answer; to be as helpful yet unobtrusive a "traffic cop" as possible; and to raise further questions by noting new angles, inconsistencies, or gaps in what students have proposed so far.

Historically it has been the teacher's role to assess student answers in discussion, but in a culture of inquiry, this is generally a mistake. Given the eventual goal of student autonomy, a gradual release of teacher responsibility is required. It must be an explicit aim, supported by your facilitation, that students become increasingly willing and able to assess contributions to the inquiry. Although you must initially model and reward such critiques, it must become a student obligation. Hence a key sign of progress is when students stop unconsciously looking at you after each student contribution, as if assessing answers (or moving the inquiry forward) were *your* role only.

In other words, inquiry is deepened only when you deliberately and transparently *avoid* teaching and judging. Your role is to facilitate more questioning and help students see the need for further inquiry—just as Socrates always did (which is why we call it Socratic questioning or a Socratic seminar).[1] Once you have asked a question and are confident that students are freely participating, your chief aim is to *listen carefully* so as to ask clarifying and probing questions about student contributions, or to make observations that remind everyone of relevant facts or previous student comments. We can say from much personal experience that you earn the greatest respect from students when you note and restate their comments better than they do.

---

[1] The Socrates of Plato's dialogues did indeed offer opinions, sometimes strongly stated ones. But the opinions were usually in response to a logically faulty view proposed by others with conviction, which led eventually back to a reconsideration of those views once the questionable logic was exposed by Socrates' questioning and discussion. The best example of this—in a famous dialogue about education—is *Meno,* for those interested in seeing Socrates at work.

In Chapter 5 we discussed numerous teacher moves to use when working with essential questions—do's and don'ts in one's role as facilitator. Here we offer a few examples of those moves to underscore this role of discerning listener and prober of student responses:

- What makes you think so, Ella? Can you show us where in the text (or problem or data) you got that idea?
- Does Jim's answer square with what you all seemed to agree to about 15 minutes ago when Joe said ___?
- Is there another way to look at this? Ramon has made a compelling case, but didn't Rosa suggest another interesting way to frame the problem?
- Do others agree? Sari, you're shaking your head no. What are your thoughts?
- How are these answers similar? How do they differ?
- Can anyone explain what you think Priscilla is getting at? (This might apply when Priscilla's comment is not clear and is in danger of being ignored even though the teacher thinks it has potential.)
- Now I'm confused. Yesterday, Ian, you said that the cause was ___, and, Tanya, you agreed. Have you guys changed your mind?

Few teachers find it easy or comfortable in the short term to listen more than speak. (That's why it helps to state a new protocol, enabling everyone—including ourselves—to be freed up to play the new game under new rules.) Indeed, one of the greatest impediments to changing the classroom culture is our own fear of things being out of control in this new role, as we discussed in Chapter 5.

The Role of the Student

Once we understand the roles of the question and of the teacher, the student's primary role comes more sharply into view. With goals now clear and "space" now provided, students must understand and practice the key role of giving voice to their ideas and gaining control of the conversation over time.

There are also misunderstandings to overcome. Discussion is not about scoring points; genuine inquiry is not a debate; false confidence in one's answers is not a virtue; too much participation is to be frowned upon if it closes off the participation of others. All these must be turned into formal rules and rubrics. Thus the role of the student is like that of an athlete: inquiry is a *team* sport in which we work together and excel when all participants contribute and are helped to do their best. And the best inquiry and discussion come from many honest and heartfelt responses, not calculated or domineering answers motivated by grades, peer pressure, or a desire to show off or dominate.

Consider these tips for making roles explicit and clear in support of a culture of inquiry:

- Watch students' eyes during a discussion. Do they unconsciously all turn back to you as soon as any student makes a contribution? Try such tactics as looking down and taking notes, reminding students of their role, or encouraging students to make at least eight consecutive contributions of either answers or questions before you chime in.

- Describe the new roles and rules in a protocol and rubric (see the next section), and practice those roles.

- Assess students' ability to ask increasingly probing and insightful questions.

- If you use written tests with writing prompts, use student quotes from prior discussions as prompts.

- Ensure that growth in addressing the essential question is assessed (e.g., through pre-tests and post-tests), whether you grade the answers or not.

Element #3: Explicit Protocols and Codes of Conduct

Given the importance of clarity about goals and roles, it follows that explicit protocols—formal codes of conduct—are essential instruments of cultural change in support of inquiry. Not only do students play a crucial role in shaping the school and classroom culture; their own subculture may (and in dysfunctional schools, often does) establish the norms and climate, thereby trumping adult beliefs and goals. For example, a common student behavioral norm is to look bored or react negatively (e.g., by rolling eyes or lobbing insults to a contributor about a grade-grubbing motive). Only deliberate attention to a code of conduct and reinforcement of it can counter such forces.

In fact, the whole point of certain instructional approaches such as question-answer-relationship (QAR), Socratic seminar, literature circles, science labs, and problem- and project-based learning—as well as rules in all games and sports—is to deliberately signal via protocols, language, and tools that desired results are best accomplished by adopting and mastering a set of explicit procedures.

The power of using questioning protocols is not limited to academic institutions. In fact, successful companies use such protocols for developing a questioning culture, as revealed in these comments from Eric Schmidt, head of Google:

We run the company by questions, not by answers. So in the strategy process we've so far formulated 30 questions that we have to answer. I'll give you an example: we have a lot of cash. What should we do with the cash? . . . How do we make that product produce better content, not just lots of content? An interesting question . . . What are the next big breakthroughs in search? And the competitive questions: What do we do about the various products Microsoft is allegedly offering? You ask it as a question, rather than a pithy answer, and that stimulates conversation. Out of the conversation comes innovation. Innovation is not something that I just wake up one day and say "I want to innovate." I think you get a better innovative culture if you ask it as a question. (Caplan, 2006)

Recall that Grant treated group inquiry as a team sport. He identified explicit moves and roles that needed to be taken on, practiced, and improved. The teacher facilitation questions, identified earlier, for example, were put on handouts and placards. Students were told that their job was to learn those moves: "These questions are not just *my* moves. They have to become *yours,* as quickly as possible, because the quality of the discussion depends upon it. I will ask you to take on and practice these roles over the next few weeks. By the end of the year, you are expected to use them naturally." Students were also invited in later years to formulate the rules of good discussion and uphold them. Indeed, one year the students proposed and implemented a penalty box as in hockey, where you could be sent by consensus (or by a classmate deemed a good "ref") for a two-minute "misconduct" that required you to be silent!

These protocols are needed because we are all guilty of sometimes falling back on habits such as talking too much, being sarcastic, or closing off inquiry when we get an answer we like. We need such formal codes of conduct to make us more deliberate and self-conscious about avoiding natural but unhelpful behaviors and language.

Here are tips for developing protocols and a code of conduct in support of a culture of inquiry:

• Work with students to develop a draft code of conduct for in-class discussion of essential questions.

• Teach students the moves that you are making as facilitator and thus the moves you want them to take on. Ask them to try one or two of those moves each day, in the same way we do it in athletics: practice the moves first in drills and then apply them in a genuine performance.

• Ask students to take on roles that they feel most comfortable assuming or in which they have an interest. Set aside specific periods of time in which they try out those roles in discussion. Ask them to self-assess each time. Regularly review with the class how well everyone is doing individually and collectively in playing the roles needed for successful inquiry.

Element #4: Safe and Supportive Environment

If participants don't feel safe, part of a team, or that their contribution is valued; if students fear looking stupid because both teacher and peer comments tend to feed insecurity; if teacher grading systems reward factual knowledge only, then it doesn't matter what teachers say about inquiry or even what the official code of conduct is. When confronted with a nonsupportive climate, students will simply not take many public risks, as reflected in quiet, safe questions; posturing and false confidence in their words; and no apparent willingness to question the teacher, the content, or one another.

A primary way to signal the proper climate for inquiry comes from the deliberate modeling of honest uncertainty. We must overcome in ourselves—and help students overcome—the fear of looking and sounding foolish in expressions of uncertainty. That fear runs deep in both teachers and students, so that even the invitation to freely inquire and discuss essential questions is rarely embraced initially. Indeed, over the decades, the two of us have often observed that many of the *best* student, and even adult, ideas have been preceded by a revealing preface: "I know this sounds stupid, but . . ."

Thus it is imperative that we give voice to the problem of doubt, uncertainty, and fear of sounding foolish. Positive changes in climate are evident when teachers and students start noting explicitly that, in spite of speakers' fears, the "dumb" comments may invariably prove insightful or spark worthwhile ideas.

It is thus also imperative that some time be devoted to a discussion of the current climate and what might be done to improve it, either in class discussion or through student surveys. Figure 6.2 shows a simple survey that Grant used every week.

As we noted in Chapter 4, there are a variety of teacher moves for advancing inquiry and discussion. On the flip side is a long-known set of inappropriate teacher behaviors that will inhibit thinking, sharing, and exploration of answers and ideas. But from a cultural perspective there are other environmental elements that can support (or undercut) the moves made by teachers in helping students speak freely and honestly about their ideas.

Try these ideas for developing a safe and inviting climate for individual contributions in support of a culture of inquiry:

- Review the ideas mentioned in Chapter 4.
- Videotape or audiotape your class for a few days. First, listen to yourself— your tone of voice, your wait time. Count the number of higher-order versus lower-order questions you ask. Listen to your reactions to student comments. What helps or hinders a level of comfort for students in your manner? Now listen to and watch students. What key moves elicit or inhibit thoughtful comments and in-depth inquiry? What feedback and protocols are thus suggested for establishing a safe and supportive culture in your classes moving forward?
- Appoint one or more "process observers" to use an established rubric or a checklist to take notes and give feedback following discussions.

Element #5: Use of Space and Physical Resources

Free-flowing, extended, and in-depth discussion is far easier if the space is configured to support it. Every teacher knows that putting people in circles or rectangles facilitates better conversation than if they are in rows looking at the

Figure 6.2 Class Climate Survey

1. How did you feel about today's discussion?					
	1	2	3	4	
2. How was the treatment of issues?					
Deep	1	2	3	4	Superficial
3. How open and honest were the class discussions?					
Open, free, honest talk	1	2	3	4	Cautious, phony talk
4. How comfortable/safe did you feel?					
Safe	1	2	3	4	Afraid to speak my mind
5. How was the facilitator?					
Great listener	1	2	3	4	Poor listener/ too much talk
Skilled control	1	2	3	4	Not in control
6. What were the highlights of the discussion? _____					
_____					
7. What were the low points of the discussion? _____					
_____					
8. Comments: _____					
_____					

backs of heads and only facing the teacher. As Adler (1983) said, a prerequisite for successful dialogue "is the furniture of the room," which should be "the antithesis of the lecture hall" (p. 173). As the authors of *The Paideia Classroom* put it, "the rationale for the seminar circle is to make it easier for all students to address their classmates," and the teacher should sit in the circle so that she "does not assume, symbolically, the role of authority figure" (Roberts & Billings, 1999, pp. 53, 56).

Most modern companies, especially in Silicon Valley, have experimented with a wide array of configurations of space and furniture to maximize conversations and innovation. Here is a telling story about what Steve Jobs demanded when the new Pixar headquarters was being built:

He had the Pixar building designed to promote unplanned encounters and collaborations. "If a building doesn't encourage that, you'll lose a lot of innovation and the magic that's sparked by serendipity," he said. "So we designed the building to make people get out of their offices and mingle in the central atrium with people they might not otherwise see." The front doors and main stairs and corridors all led to the atrium; the café and the mailboxes were there, the conference rooms had windows that looked out onto it; and the 600-seat theater and 2 smaller screening rooms all spilled into it. "Steve's theory worked from day one," Lasseter recalls. "I kept running into people I hadn't seen for months. I've never seen a building that promoted collaboration and creativity as well as this one." (Isaacson, 2012, p. 100)

Admittedly, most of us do not have the opportunity to design our schools, but most teachers have considerable control over their classroom space in this era of movable and modular furniture. We encourage you to do an analysis of how classroom furnishings might be altered to make clear that inquiry, discussion, and collaboration are key experiences in your room. (For a rich online report about the design of educational spaces, see http://jan.ucc.nau.edu/lrm22/learning_spaces/; and for an interesting article on the design of workspace from an architectural perspective, go to http://www.archdaily.com/215703/caring-for-your-office-introvert/.)

Try these tips for developing a supportive space and for using furnishings to support a culture of inquiry:

• Move student desks or chairs into circles or rectangles when collaborative inquiry is the goal.

• If you have an extremely large class, it may be necessary to have an inner circle and an outer circle in which half the class takes turns discussing while the other half takes notes and is prepared to later comment on both the content and the process of the discussion. Alternately, you can have small-group discussions as part of learning stations.

Element #6: Use of Time in and out of Class

Throughout this book we have asked readers to explicitly set aside defined times in which collaborative inquiry into questions is expected to happen, so as to signal a shift in goals and means. Although any percentage we might propose would be arbitrary, we can say that a sensible range might be somewhere between 20 and 50 percent of your class time with students being devoted to in-depth collaborative inquiry. The greatest fallacy in our field—what we dub the "egocentric fallacy" of education—is "If I taught it and highlighted it, then they must have learned it (or should have)." The corollary is "Too much time in discussion and reflection takes away from precious time needed to cover all the material." What we now know scientifically— what all good teachers know intuitively—is that time is needed for processing complicated ideas. Indeed, if we care about student understanding, then it is imperative that we allocate class time for meaning-making; for ongoing assessments to tease out confusions and misunderstandings; and to permit metacognitive insights about how to better inquire, discuss, and learn. As one example, consider Eric Mazur, a professor of physics at Harvard University who has compiled research for more than a decade to show that greater understanding and technical knowledge (as measured by conventional tests as well as tests of misconceptions related to physics) can result from *less* formal teaching and *more* peer interaction and constructivist learning experiences (Mazur, 1997). His instructional effectiveness is especially noteworthy given that he conducts large classes in a lecture hall. He is also one of the pioneers in higher education of the use of pupil-response systems (clickers) to actively involve all students and regularly monitor their understanding (see a video of Mazur's method in action at http://www.youtube.com/watch?v=lBYrKPoVFwg).

It is not just the time *in* class that must be considered. What we ask students to do outside class is arguably as important in achieving inquiry-related goals. No substantive discussion of a text, issue, or set of data can occur if students haven't read a text, done an experiment, engaged in Internet research, or explored and shared ideas in study groups.

Whatever one thinks of the quality of the videos in the Khan Academy (www.khanacademy.org), it is absolutely clear that the idea of "flipping" the classroom is here to stay—and thankfully so. With a world of information, tutorials, and virtual feedback easily available to everyone *outside* class, precious class minutes can now be devoted to arguably the best use of our time together: sharing ideas, applying knowledge to worthy tasks, getting and using feedback, and reflecting on lingering questions (see Bergmann & Sams, 2012; Miller, 2012).

Consider the following tips for ways to optimize the use of time in support of a culture of inquiry:

• With your colleagues, consider the following question: What's the best use of precious time in class, and out of class, to accomplish learning goals?

• Set aside a formal time period in which pursuit of questions by students is the task at hand, for which protocols and codes of conduct have been formally established, and in which some time is provided to learn and practice new roles related to the goal.

• Time should also be set aside routinely for a debriefing of inquiry and discussion—*What worked? What didn't? What were the highlights? What needs improvement?*—just as coaches do with athletes and performing artists.

Element #7: Use of Texts and Other Learning Resources

Throughout this book (and throughout all of our writings on teaching for understanding), we have cautioned readers to think of the textbook as a resource, not the curriculum. For, as we noted in discussing Element #1, when the curriculum is the textbook and teachers march through it, the message is clear and inexorable; that is, the point of school is to learn stuff that is handed to you. In a textbook-driven classroom, in-depth inquiry is thus felt to be tangential, an *inefficient* use of time given that there is so much material to cover. So teachers have to be proactive in looking at just what the textbook can and cannot do to further inquiry. In most cases that requires providing additional resources that make up for what the textbook lacks— for example, a syllabus, additional text and media resources, written protocols, individual and group research projects, and (especially) inquiry-focused assessments and rubrics.

Here is a simple example, in U.S. history, of how to supplement a textbook. Suppose you want students to consider the following EQ: *Whose history is it? What is objective and what is bias in history?* Alas, most textbooks gloss over the matter and ironically set themselves up as authoritative sources—often in a way that obscures when they are pushing a particular understanding as opposed to merely presenting facts. (For more on this critical issue, see *Lies My Teacher Told Me: Everything Your American History Textbook Got Wrong,* by James Loewen 1996.)

Here is a brief additional reading, concerning the American Revolution, that could supplement the one in a current textbook and allow students to explore the EQs in greater depth:

What then were the causes of the American Revolution? It used to be argued that the Revolution was caused by the tyranny of the British government in the years following the Seven Years War. This view is no longer acceptable. Historians now recognize that the British colonies were the freest in the world. . . .

The French menace was removed after 1763 and the colonies no longer felt dependent on England's aid. This did not mean that they wished for independence. The great majority of the colonists were loyal, even after the Stamp Act. They were proud of the Empire and its liberties. . . . In the years following the Stamp Act a small minority of radicals began to work for independence. They watched for every opportunity of stirring up trouble. . . . The radicals immediately seized the opportunity of making a crisis and in Boston it was this group who staged the Boston Tea Party. . . . In the Thirteen Colonies the Revolution had really been a civil war in which the whole population was torn with conflicting loyalties. John Adams later said that in 1776 probably not more than one-third of the people favored war. (U.S. Department of Health, Education, and Welfare, 1976, p. 17)

As you may have suspected, this is not from a typical U.S. textbook. But it *is* from a high school history textbook—from Canada! Now the questions—*What is history? Whose story? Which sources can you trust?*—all come to life as a result of a simple supplement to the main textbook. (Note, too, how the example embodies the idea we introduced in Chapter 4, whereby we confront students with alternative points of view for the essential question.)

We strongly recommend that teachers use the following set of questions to look carefully at each textbook to see if (and where) it has enough of what is needed to support a culture of inquiry. Given the essential question,

- What chapters should be highlighted? Skimmed? Skipped entirely?
- What sections of the chapter should be highlighted? Skimmed? Skipped entirely?
- What parts of the chapter need to be supplemented with resources that highlight alternative points of view, contemporary issues, or "messy" problems?
- What important questions lurk under the glib summary?
- What information related to the EQ is unavailable in the chapter?
- What assessments have to be designed to address the EQ, especially when the textbook quizzes only highlight content to be mastered?

Element #8: Assessment Practices

Last but not least, a key aspect of any educational culture has to do with the assessments. These old truisms contain much wisdom: "We measure what we value"; "What gets measured gets done"; and "If we count it, it counts." Of course, students are quick to pick up on this aspect of the school game, as evidenced by their constant queries: "Will this be on the test?" "Does this count?" "How many points is this worth?" If we test and grade it, it's important; if we don't assess it, it simply won't be seen as important (no matter how much we *say* we value it).

Almost no textbook or district assessment sends a clear and unambiguous message that in-depth inquiry into important questions really matters. So any hope of changing beliefs, attitudes, and behaviors concerning thinking and inquiry will require us to develop assessments that practice what essential questions preach.

Simply stated, we must assess the student's ability to question, to probe, and to respond to high-level questions with evidence and argument. Indeed, these are priorities in the new Common Core State Standards for English/language arts. (A more thorough discussion of assessment appears in our other works on Understanding by Design [see Wiggins & McTighe, 2005, 2011, & 2012].)

A natural way to use essential questions in assessments is to pose the question multiple times as a formal prompt. Ask the EQ as a pre-assessment, in ongoing formative assessments, and as a part of a summative assessment. Because the aim is better questioning and answering, this simple technique makes crystal clear what we are looking for. Then, make clear via rubrics and work samples the nature of the progress you seek.

An elegant trick that Grant has used in his teaching to emphasize that discussion and careful listening matter is to occasionally have a "matching quotes" quiz, using quotes that came from the in-class discussion. The quiz requires matching the quote with the topic under discussion and the student who said it. In a related strategy, Grant's daughter, Alexis, has developed coding systems (Figure 6.3) for monitoring and assessing student discussions in real time. (You can see her students in action, engaging in an in-depth discussion of *Romeo and Juliet* with no teacher intervention of any kind, at www.authenticeducation.org/alexis.) Here is a version of a document that Alexis used when she was a teacher in New York:

Because this is a team effort, there will be a team grade. The whole class will get the same grade. This is what you need to do, as a class, to earn an *A:*

A truly hard-working, analytical discussion in which—

1. *Everyone* has participated in a meaningful and substantive way, and more or less equally.
2. The pace allows for clarity and thoughtfulness—but not boredom.
3. There is a sense of balance and order; focus is on one speaker at a time and one idea at a time. The discussion is lively without being "hyper" or superficial.
4. The discussion builds. There is an attempt to resolve questions and issues before moving on to new ones.
5. Comments are not lost; the loud or verbose do not dominate; the shy or quiet are encouraged.
6. Students listen carefully and respectfully to one another. There is no talking, daydreaming, rustling papers, making faces, using phones or laptops, etc., when someone else is speaking (this communicates disrespect and undermines the discussion as a whole). Same goes for sarcastic and glib comments.
7. Everyone is clearly understood. Those who are not heard or understood are urged to repeat.
8. Students take risks and dig for deep meaning, new insights.
9. Students back up what they say with examples, quotations, etc. Students ask others to back up assertions with proof (if possible). The text is referred to often.

The class will earn an *A* by doing all of this at an impressively high level (very rare). The class will earn a *B* by doing most things on this list (a pretty good discussion). The class will earn a *C* for doing half or slightly more than half of what's on this list. The class earns a *D* by doing less than half of what's on the list. The class earns an *F* if the discussion is a real mess or a complete dud and virtually nothing on this list is accomplished or genuinely attempted. Unprepared or unwilling students will bring the group down as a whole. Please remember this as you read, take notes, and prepare for class discussion.

Figure 6.3 Sample Coding Tool for Group Discussions (Secondary Level)

★ = Insightful comment
A = Abrupt shift, cuts off conversation flow
C^D = Connection to previous class discussion
C^L = Connection to life
C^{OT} = Connection to outside text
C^T = Connection to current text (not reading passage)
C^W = Connection to what's on board
D = Distracted, talking, off task
E = Explanation
EQ = Reference to course/unit essential question
F = Surface or summary observation
G = Glib, silly, or sarcastic comment
H = Hard to hear
H^C = Asked to speak up
I = Interruption
IG = Illogical statement or prediction
IG^Q = Illogical question
L = Lost comment
O = Organizing, leading, or calling for order
O^{SP} = Puts someone on spot
P = Prediction
Q = Question
Q^2 = Level 2 question
$Q^★$ = Insightful question
Q^C = Clarifying question
Q^F = Surface question
R = Rambling, unfocused, going on and on without clear, pithy point
Rp = Repeating exact point someone else made (didn't hear it previously)
S = Reference to author/writing style
Sp = Put on the spot by classmate(s)
T = Reference to the text
W = Writes something on board
X = Error in comprehension
X^C = Correction of error
Y = Synthesizes, sees big picture

Source: © 2013 Alexis Wiggins. Used by permission.

In addition, Figures 6.3 and 6.4 are practical tools that you can use or modify to monitor group discussions by coding observable behaviors and to signal to learners what and how you will assess.

Here are tips for developing assessments in support of inquiry and discussion:

• Provide individuals, small groups, and the entire class with regular feedback on how their behavior aligns with the goals and criteria in support of collaborative inquiry using the resources provided in the examples in this chapter.

• Videotape your class every so often, and have students self-assess their performance using the rubrics or coding sheets you provide them.

• Ensure that part of your grading system includes the student's development as a questioner and as a participant in collaborative inquiries.

Figure 6.4 Sample Coding Tools for Group Discussions (Elementary Level)

Group discussion	Not Yet	Sometimes	Usually	Mostly	Always
Everyone participated.					
Everyone listened attentively.					
Everyone spoke loudly and clearly.					
Everyone stayed on topic.					

You can simplify coding for individual students by adapting a seating chart that is arranged to match your classroom. A mock-up of a traditional classroom arrangement is provided, but not necessarily recommended.

Key: * = Contribution   I = Interruption   Q = Relevant Question   D = Distracted, talking, off task

Front of classroom

Form Follows Function

As we noted earlier in this chapter, we can summarize all the ideas here in the maxims "walk the talk" and "practice what you preach." The classroom environment and agenda should be shaped to ensure that the practices and the policies align with the goal of effective inquiry.

In Figure 6.5, we summarize the eight elements that support a culture of inquiry and questioning contrasted with those factors that can undermine it. Think of these eight elements as criteria by which you can self-assess your own classroom or school, and use them to guide your actions and any needed adjustments moving forward.

Figure 6.5 Eight Controllable Classroom Culture Elements

Cultural Element	Conditions That Support a Questioning Culture	Conditions That Undermine a Questioning Culture
1. Nature of the learning goals	Students recognize the *various* kinds of learning goals, especially that inquiry into open-ended questions is different from (but as important as) the goal of content mastery.	Students believe (with reinforcement because of teacher actions) that the point of learning is solely mastery of content knowledge. Students believe that teacher questions are after *the* answer and that extended inquiry and discussion, no matter how intellectually engaging, are distractions from or not related to the real goal.
2. Role of questions, teachers, and students	Teacher and student roles are explicitly defined to support collective inquiry into essential questions. Active intellectual engagement and meaning-making are expected of the student. Essential questions serve as touchstones, and answers are to be questioned.	The teacher assumes the role of expert, and the student is expected to be a willing recipient of knowledge. Questions are used to probe students' grasp of material, and answers are either correct or incorrect.
3. Explicit protocols and codes of conduct	There are explicit protocols and a code of conduct for appropriate behavior related to asking questions and responding to questions and answers. All learners are expected to participate and contribute, and all contributions will be treated with respect.	There is no explicit protocol or code of conduct for how to engage in inquiry and discussion, or how to respond to teacher questions or student answers. The teacher routinely calls only on students who volunteer, so that student passivity and disengagement are tacitly accepted.
4. Safe and supportive environment	The teacher establishes and models a safe and supportive climate for intellectual risk-taking and challenges to ideas. Inappropriate behaviors (for example, put-downs) are firmly but tactfully addressed.	The teacher fails to model and reinforce the climate necessary for helping students feel safe and willing to take intellectual risks. Students may be made to feel stupid or inadequate.
5. Use of space and physical resources	Essential questions are prominently posted or otherwise visible and referred to regularly. Classroom furniture and use of space are deliberately organized to support free-flowing, engaged, and respectful conversation.	The arrangement of furniture prevents everyone from seeing each other in the class. Neither teacher nor students take steps to rearrange the setup to support group inquiry; thus sustained discussion is undercut.

Figure 6.5 *(continued)*

Cultural Element	Conditions That Support a Questioning Culture	Conditions That Undermine a Questioning Culture
6. Use of time in and out of class	Time is explicitly devoted to formal explorations of essential questions. Out-of-class assignments include project- and problem-based inquiry around the questions.	Time is not specifically allocated for inquiry and in-depth discussion. The teacher uses class time to present content material primarily through direct or didactic instruction. Homework is directed toward review, practice, or reading for acquisition only.
7. Use of texts and other learning resources	Texts and other support materials are chosen to advance inquiry. The teacher makes it clear that textbooks and related resources are limited in their ability to drive inquiry into essential questions.	The textbook is treated as the syllabus rather than a supportive resource. Teachers march through the text sequentially, making it seem as if coverage matters more than inquiry.
8. Assessment practices	Summative assessments and associated rubrics reflect the essential questions. Open-ended assessment tasks honor inquisitiveness and critical thinking, whereas traditional measures are used to assess important knowledge and skills.	Summative assessments, associated rubrics, and grades focus on mastery of content knowledge and skills. Students quickly see that "what counts" is recall and recognition.

7

How Do We Use Essential Questions Beyond the Classroom?

The focus of this book has been on what teachers can do to improve the quality of inquiry and intellectual engagement in *their* classrooms. However, the culture of the larger organization (school and district or university) surely influences the behavior of staff and students. Accordingly, we conclude with a consideration of ways in which policymakers, district and school administrators, and teacher leaders can contribute to an institutional ethos that encourages professional inquiry into matters of learning, teaching, curriculum, assessment, and concomitant school policies and structures.

Using Essential Questions with Staff and Colleagues

One straightforward and practical method for encouraging an organizational culture of questioning is to regularly use essential questions with staff and colleagues. Principals, department chairpersons, and team leaders can naturally "walk the talk" by framing important initiatives, committee work, and faculty/team meetings around recurring EQs. In fact, the same thought experiment applied to academic content applies to school and district matters: if a targeted initiative or program is viewed as an "answer," what are the questions? For example, if *differentiated instruction* or *curriculum mapping* is being advocated by school or district leaders, what problems is each expected to solve? Are there other approaches that might also (or perhaps better) address the identified needs or problems?

Throughout our long careers, we have witnessed numerous cases in which worthwhile school- and district-level reforms failed to take root or endure because leaders assumed that teachers would embrace them on face value. Indeed, it is often the failure to make the case for the reform that dooms an initiative. How many times have we heard veteran educators dismiss a staff development topic or new initiative as "this year's new thing" or reflect a "this too shall pass" attitude? In other words, *unless* staff and other constituents understand the need for a change and its implications for their work, it is less likely to be embraced and enacted with fidelity.

This principle applies to our own work. We never recommend that school leaders simply mandate Understanding by Design (UbD). Rather, UbD must come to be seen as the answer to such questions as these: *What are the most persistent and important student performance deficits? Why do our students have such trouble in doing higher-order work and in transferring their learning? To what extent are our students engaged? Do they perceive that they are involved in meaningful schoolwork? What initiatives are therefore suggested by this analysis?* UbD can only take root and be seen as a natural solution to problems we acknowledge if it is seen as an answer to honest questions we have posed and considered as a staff.

Essential questions can thus play a critical role in making school reform be better understood, embraced, and enacted with fidelity. Rather than jumping right into an implementation action plan, savvy leaders can pose EQs to engage staff in exploring the need for various initiatives and associated solutions. Here are examples of essential questions that have been used to engage staff in collaborative inquiries resulting in greater understanding of, and dedication to, enacting needed reforms.

The Mission of Schooling

• To what extent does our (team, school, district, community) share a common mission?

• To what extent do our policies, priorities, and actions honor our mission?

• Are we adequately preparing learners for life in the 21st century?

Beliefs About Teaching and Learning

• What educational beliefs about teaching and learning do we hold? Are all those beliefs supported by research, best practice, and our own experience?

• What assumptions about learning guide our instructional and assessment practices?

• To what extent do our policies, priorities, and actions reflect these beliefs?

• To what extent do our beliefs about learning align with our practices?

Standards

• How would people know that we are a "standards-based" school or district?

• To what extent are we "walking the talk" in using standards to guide our work (e.g., curriculum, assessment, instruction, professional development, staff appraisal)?

Curriculum

• Is our curriculum truly planned backward from our long-term goals and priorities?

• To what extent is our curriculum coherent and aligned—from the learners' perspective?

- To what extent does our current curriculum support inquiry, transfer, and authentic performance?
- What content should we "cover" and what needs to be "uncovered?"
- For what do we need textbooks? Why? If so, how should they be used?

Assessment

- How are we doing? What's working, what's not?
- What evidence is needed to answer these questions, and do we have it? If we don't, where might we find more credible, valid, and accepted evidence?
- How will we know that students really understand?
- Are we assessing everything we value or only those things that are most easily tested and graded?
- Is anything important falling through the cracks because we are not assessing it?
- How might our assessments promote learning, not simply measure it?

Instruction

- To what extent is our instruction engaging and effective?
- To what extent does our instruction reflect research and best practices?
- To what extent are we engaging students in "doing" the subject?
- Are we effectively reaching all students, especially low achievers?

Professional Development

- To what extent do our professional development practices reflect our learning principles?
- How does our staff really view professional development?
- To what extent are our professional development practices results oriented?
- Is our professional development appropriately differentiated?

Change Process

- What do we believe about educational change? To what extent are these beliefs shared? To what extent are these beliefs supported by research?
- To what extent are various initiatives seen as connected and coherent (as opposed to being seen as separate things or "add-ons")?
- How might we "work smarter" and more effectively?

Policy and Structures

- To what extent do our policies, structures, and culture reflect our beliefs about learning?
- How might we restructure to enhance learning?
- What is the best use of our time when teachers are not with students?
- What messages do our policies send?
- To what extent is our current staff appraisal process working?
- What is a culture of continuous improvement? To what extent do we have one?
- What existing factors support this (priority initiative)? What factors resist change?

- How do our staff and leaders receive the honest feedback they need to improve?
- To what extent do our grading and reporting practices communicate clearly, honestly, and fairly?
- Are resources (e.g., time, money, facilities, technology) being used optimally to advance learning?

Other

- Would you want *your* child to attend *our* school? What, specifically, might give you pause, and why?
- How boring is the average day, from the students' perspective? How much of that boredom is unnecessary—a consequence of less than ideal practices on our part?
- Where do unthinking habits and rituals get in the way of a better education?

Understandably, educational leaders may harbor concerns that the process of involving staff in deliberations and (sometimes messy) discussions and debates will take too long and allow the saboteurs to better organize to derail the effort. Over the years we have heard the predictable "yes, buts"—"That's all well and good, but we have to get things done"; "You don't understand; we're under the gun"; "People will just talk forever if we let them"; "We've got deadlines to meet"; and so on.

We acknowledge that examining an issue in intellectually honest ways using essential questions will take longer than simply mandating actions. Certainly, leaders can simply issue directives (and there are times when rule by fiat may be necessary), but mandates rarely engender understanding and commitment among professionals, and sometimes they have the opposite effect. We liken the challenge to the one that virtually every teacher faces; that is, there is lots of content to cover, and it would be so much quicker if we just talked fast in class! But the most effective teachers understand that unless the students are engaged and come to *understand through active meaning-making,* their learning will likely be superficial, not enduring. We believe the situation is similar with staff and constituents. Worthy initiatives require inquiry-based meetings in order for staff to understand and take ownership of the *why* and the *how* of proposed initiatives. Essential questions provide the vehicle for the kind of focused and rich professional conversations needed to inspire dedicated implementation.

Using Essential Questions with Professional Learning Communities

A growing number of educators are involved in professional learning communities (PLCs), and the PLC structure clearly offers potential for making inquiry more deliberately central to the adults in schools. Indeed, we contend that one of the most intellectually engaging and effective uses of PLCs are related to collaborative inquiries into the persistent challenges of teaching and deficits of performance. In this regard, we have described three primary roles for teachers and administrators in PLC groups: (1) critical friends, (2) analysts of student work, and (3) action researchers (McTighe, 2008). Here is a summary of these roles, with corresponding questions.

Critical Friends

Most teachers plan lessons and units of study based on an established framework of national, state, or district standards. However, teacher-developed curriculum plans are often created in isolation and are rarely reviewed by administrators (with the exception of plans prepared by untenured novices) or colleagues. Moreover, teachers can sometimes get too close to their work and have difficulty seeing any weaknesses. PLC groups offer an antidote to these problems by offering educators opportunities for collaborative planning and serving as critical friends to review each other's unit plans, lessons, and assessments. Simply put, working in teams to plan curricula and offer helpful reviews reduces teacher isolation while enhancing instructional effectiveness.

Unfortunately, collegial feedback is not the norm in many schools. Indeed, some schools unwittingly support a "go it alone" ethos that translates academic freedom into "let me close my door and do my thing." Even in collaborative school cultures, educators tend to avoid criticizing each other's professional practices. Yet we know feedback is necessary for improvement. Honest, specific, and descriptive feedback from peers can be invaluable to beginners as well as veteran teachers. Accordingly, we recommend that structured opportunities for peer reviews of each others' curriculum plans be included as a formal aspect of professional learning communities.

Of course, any collegial review process should be guided by an agreed-upon protocol and set of review criteria so that the feedback is standards based and depersonalized. *The Understanding by Design Guide to Advanced Concepts in Creating and Reviewing Units* (Wiggins & McTighe, 2012) contains a module describing such a structured peer review process based on explicit design standards. It is in this context of collegial reviews that reflective questions can be applied. Here are sample questions to use in structuring peer feedback and guidance for unit plans:

To what extent does the unit plan

- Align with relevant standards, mission, or program goals?
- Point toward long-term transfer goals involving genuine performance?
- Focus on important, transferable ideas?
- Identify relevant, open-ended, and thought-provoking essential questions?
- Contain assessments that provide valid and sufficient evidence of all identified goals?
- Include authentic performance tasks requiring transfer?
- Include appropriate evaluative criteria or rubrics for open-ended assessments?

- Contain learning events and instruction to help learners achieve identified unit goals?
  - Coherently align all activities and assessments with unit goals?

After several opportunities to receive peer feedback, as well as to assume the role of critical friend, teachers begin to internalize these questions and become more deliberate in their own unit planning. It has also been our experience that once the benefits of helpful feedback and guidance in a safe PLC environment are realized, teachers are likely to seek more peer interaction of this type.

Analysts of Student Work

Across the globe, educators are being encouraged to use student performance data as a basis for instructional decision making and school improvement planning. Often, however, the data come exclusively from the results of an external (e.g., state or national) test. Although these standardized assessments certainly provide some data on student achievement, such an annual snapshot is not sufficiently detailed or timely enough to inform and guide continuous improvement actions at the classroom and school levels. A more robust approach to school improvement calls for staff to engage in an *ongoing* analysis of overall student performance, examining a *range* of credible data from multiple sources. What is needed, metaphorically speaking, is a photo album of evidence—results from traditional tests *along with* a collection of student work generated from common assignments and varied assessment tasks.

When teachers meet in role-alike PLC teams (e.g., by grade level and subject areas) to evaluate the results from assessments, they begin to identify general patterns of strengths as well as areas needing improvement. We have previously published questions to guide the evaluation and analysis of student work and the planned adjustments to improve the results (Wiggins & McTighe, 2007). Consider these:

- Are these the results we expected? Why or why not?
- Are there any surprises? Any anomalies?
- What does this work reveal about student learning and performance?
- What patterns of strengths and weaknesses are evident?
- What misconceptions are revealed?
- How good is "good enough" (e.g., the performance standard)?
- What action(s) at the teacher, team, school, and district levels would improve learning and performance?

By regularly using such questions to examine student work, teachers properly focus on the broader learning goals (including understanding, transfer, habits of mind), while avoiding a fixation on standardized test scores. The regular use of such a collaborative process provides the fuel for continuous improvement while establishing a professionally enriching, results-oriented culture.

Action Researchers

One particularly robust form of professional inquiry is action research (AR). Action research involves ongoing, collaborative investigations into matters of teaching and learning, and it is well suited to a PLC structure. The action research process empowers teams to identify problems and shape solutions while fostering a culture of a collegial approach to school improvement. It operates under the assumption that local educators, not only outside experts, know best about where and how to improve their schools. Unlike the (sometimes) esoteric research studies conducted in universities by degree-pursuing students or by faculty members needing to publish, action research projects are initiated and conducted by teams of practicing educators, and the projects focus on relevant learning issues.

At its root, action research offers a structured process for professional inquiry. Here is a summary of a seven-step process for AR:

1. Identify an issue, a problem, a challenge, or an anomaly related to teaching or learning that is particularly interesting or puzzling to you and your team, and linked to an essential question. For example:

    EQ: *How well do our students think? How might we enhance their critical thinking skills and habits?*

    Challenge: We have observed that 8th graders are generally not critical thinkers; that is, it is difficult to get them to understand when and how they are being persuaded or manipulated by what they see and hear.

2. Once you have selected the issue, generate a more focused inquiry question.

    Example: How can we develop a sequence of learning activities using a variety of texts and media examples that will help 8th graders recognize various persuasive techniques; learn how to think more critically about what they read, hear, and see; and learn how to avoid being manipulated?

3. Form a hypothesis.

    Example: Using a variety of texts and media, along with guided instruction (e.g., analysis of persuasive techniques and critical-thinking protocols), we can improve students' critical-thinking capacities.

4. Given the hypothesis, identify relevant data you will collect. Selecting data from several relevant sources (triangulation) will enable more valid inferences.

    Example: We will create performance tasks that ask students to critically appraise print and media sources (e.g., advertisements, letters to the editor, political campaign commercials, and other persuasive texts), and judge their responses using a critical-thinking rubric. We will use informal think-alouds to listen to students' analyses of persuasive techniques and their influences. We will assess using a section of the Ennis-Weir Critical

Thinking Test. We will have students create a persuasive piece using one or more designated persuasive techniques and judge their work using a rubric on persuasion.

5. Collect, organize, and represent the data.

6. Analyze the data. Look for patterns. Interpret the results. What does this mean? What do the results tell us?

7. Summarize your findings. Given what we have learned, what actions will we take? What new questions emerged? What new inquiries might we undertake?

Of course, not all action research projects in your school or PLC need to follow such a formal process. In fact, we recommend beginning with one or more simpler inquiries, such as those listed in Figure 7.1.

When schools and teacher teams employ EQs to examine proposed initiatives, engage in critical-friend peer reviews, examine student work in teams, and conduct action research inquiries, they are walking the talk—a hallmark of true professionalism.

As the varied suggestions in Figure 7.1 indicate, the overall culture of the school can be substantially improved by a deliberate attempt to shape adult conversation in the school via EQs. Moreover, the recommendations we have made in the previous chapters about implementing EQs have their obvious parallels in adult interactions. For example, the summary of factors in Figure 6.5 (pp. 100–101) also apply to establishing an organizational culture of questioning.

Conclusion

We suggest that you be humble yet resolute. Fully embedding essential questions, and an inquiry focus more generally, into classroom and school life will likely require a significant shift in norms and actions. As we have noted throughout these chapters, there must be an assertive molding of classroom and organizational culture because the desired conditions rarely occur naturally in a world where traditional roles, staff isolation, unprioritized curricula, coverage-focused teaching (and thus student passivity), test-prep pressures, and grading practices take time-honored precedence. Fortunately there are expectations, structures, and pedagogies that can be put in place to make a culture of inquiry more likely. Such a culture happens, therefore, when educators act in purposeful, perceptive, and persistent ways to identify those unhelpful traditions and replace them with inquiry-supportive routines.

Figure 7.1 Ideas for Getting Started with Action Research Around EQs

Shadow a Student
What's the student's real experience?   Pick a student at random and follow that student for a day. As you "walk in the student's shoes," consider questions such as these: *Is the schoolwork engaging? Boring? Do the learners see purpose and relevance in what they are learning? Are they exploring big ideas? What are your impressions of their school experiences?* Take notes and report on your observations and reflections at the next faculty or PLC meeting.
Monitor Questioning Strategies
How well do we question?   Monitor your use of classroom questioning. *What percentage of my questions requires factual recall? Application? Evaluation? What are the results of asking different types of questions? What happens when I use various follow-up strategies—for example, wait time, probes, devil's advocate?* Videotape yourself or visit other teachers' classrooms and take note of their questioning strategies. Then share your findings.
Replicate *A Place Called School* Study
When are students most engaged and why?   Repeat the classic John Goodlad survey as to which courses students see as most engaging (and why), as most worthwhile (and why), as most and least challenging, and so on (Goodlad, 1984). Share your findings with the rest of the faculty.
Survey Your Graduates
Are our graduates prepared?   Contact recent high school graduates. Ask them to describe the extent to which their K–12 schooling prepared them for future study and the world of work. *In what ways were they well prepared? In what ways might their schools have prepared them better?* Present and discuss survey results with teachers and administrators.
Survey Current Students
How well do students understand the point of school or class?   *Do students understand the goals and priorities?* What will students say if you ask them the following questions: *Why are you doing what you are doing? How does yesterday's lesson relate to today's? What do you predict you will be doing tomorrow? What is your long-term goal for this unit? How will your learning be judged?* Compare your findings with other teachers' findings and discuss the implications.
Examine Grading and Reporting
To what extent do grading and reporting align with (all) our goals?   Survey students and parents regarding the current grading and reporting system. *To what extent do they think grades and reports are understandable? Consistent among teachers? Fair? Accurate in communicating student performance, progress, and work habits?* Compile and report on your findings and discuss the implications for current practice.

References

Adler, M. J. (1982). *The Paideia proposal: An educational manifesto.* New York: Macmillan.

Adler, M. J. (1983). *How to speak how to listen.* New York: Collier-Macmillan.

ASCD. (2012). Understanding by design: An introduction. [PD Online course]. Alexandria, VA: Author.

Bateman, W. (1990). *Open to question: The art of teaching and learning by inquiry.* San Francisco: Jossey-Bass.

Bergmann, J., & Sams, A. (2012, April 15). How the flipped classroom is radically transforming learning [blog post]. Retrieved from http://www.thedailyriff.com/articles/how-the-flipped-classroom-is-radically-transforming-learning-536.php

Boydston, J. A. (2008). *The middle works, 1899–1924/ John Dewey.* Carbondale, IL: Southern Illinois University, p. 162.

Bruner, J. (1960). *Process of education: A landmark in educational theory.* Cambridge, MA: Harvard University Press.

Bruner, J. (1965). The growth of mind. *American Psychologist, 20*(17), 1007–1017.

Caplan, J. (2006, October 2). Google's chief looks ahead. *Time.* Retrieved from http://www.time.com/time/business/article/0,8599,1541446,00.html

Common Core State Standards Initiative. (2001). *Common Core State Standards.* Washington, DC: Council of Chief State School Officers.

Fawcett, H. (1938). The nature of proof: A description and evaluation of certain procedures used in a senior high school to develop an understanding of the nature of proof. *Tenth Yearbook of the National Council of Teachers of Mathematics* (Ch. 4). New York: Teachers College, Columbia University.

Goodlad, J. (1984). *A place called school: Prospects for the future.* New York: McGraw-Hill.

Hattie, J. (2009). *Visible learning: A synthesis of over 800 meta-analyses relating to achievement.* New York: Routledge.

Isaacson, W. (2012, April). The real leadership lessons of Steve Jobs. *Harvard Business Review, 90*(4), 92–102.

Israel, E. (2002). Examining multiple perspectives in literature. In J. Holden & J. Schmit (Eds.), *Inquiry and the literary text: Constructing discussions in the English classroom.* Urbana, IL: National Council of Teachers of English.

Krupa, M., Selman, R., & Jaquette, D. (1985). The development of science explanations in children and adolescents: A structural approach. In S. Chipman, J. Segal, & R. Glaser (Eds.), *Thinking and learning skills—Vol. 2: Research and open questions.* Hillsdale, NJ: Lawrence Erlbaum Associates.

Lemov, D. (2010). *Teach like a champion: 49 techniques that put students on the path to college.* San Francisco: Wiley.

Loewen, J. (1996). *Lies my teacher told me: Everything your American history textbook got wrong.* New York: Touchstone.

Lyman, F. (1981). The responsive classroom discussion: The inclusion of all students. In A. S. Anderson (Ed.), *Mainstreaming digest* (pp. 109–113). College Park, MD: University of Maryland.

Marzano, R., Pickering, D., & Pollock, J. (2001). *Classroom instruction that works: Research-based strategies for increasing student achievement.* Alexandria, VA: ASCD.

Mazur, E. (1997). *Peer instruction: A user's manual.* Upper Saddle River, NJ: Prentice Hall.

McTighe, J. (2008). Making the most of professional learning communities. *The Learning Principal, 3*(8), 1, 4–7.

McTighe, J., & Wiggins, G. (2004). *The Understanding by Design professional development workbook.* Alexandria, VA: ASCD.

Miller, A. (2012, February 24). Five best practices for the flipped classroom [blog post]. Retrieved from http://www.edutopia.org/blog/flipped-classroom-best-practices-andrew-miller

National Art Education Association. (1994). *National standards for arts education.* Reston, VA: Author.

National Association for Sport and Physical Education (2004). *Moving into the future: National standards for physical education* (2nd ed.). Reston, VA: Author.

Newmann, F. (1991). Promoting higher-order thinking in the teaching of social studies: Overview of a study of 16 high school departments. *Theory and Research in Social Education, 19*(4), 22–27.

Newmann, F. M. (1988, March 15). *The curriculum of thoughtful classes.* Paper presented at the annual meeting of the American Educational Research Association. New Orleans, LA.

Next Generation Science Standards. (2012). Retrieved from http://www.nextgenscience.org/

Pagliaro. M. (2011). *Exemplary classroom questioning: Practices to promote thinking and learning.* Lanham, MD: Rowman and Littlefield Education.

Palincsar, A. S., & Brown, A. L. (1984). Reciprocal teaching of comprehension-fostering and comprehension-monitoring activities. *Cognition and Instruction 1*(2), 117–175.

Pearson, P. D., & Gallagher, M. C. (1983). The instruction of reading comprehension. *Contemporary Educational Psychology, 8,* 317–344.

Polya, G. (1957). *How to solve it* (2nd ed.). Princeton, NJ: Princeton University Press.

Raphael, T. E. (1986). Teaching question-answer relationships, revisited. *The Reading Teacher, 39,* 516–522.

Roberts, T., & Billings, L. (1999). *The Paideia classroom: Teaching for understanding.* Larchmont, NY: Eye on Education.

Rothstein, D., & Santana, L. (2011). *Make just one change: Teach students to ask their own questions.* Cambridge, MA: Harvard Education Press.

Rowe, M. (1974). Relation of wait-time and rewards to the development of language, logic and fate control. Part one: Wait-time. *Journal of Research in Science Teaching, 11*(2), 81–94.

Stevenson, H., & Stigler, J. (1992). *The learning gap: Why our schools are failing and what we can learn from Japanese and Chinese education.* New York: Touchstone.

Tobin, K., & Capie, W. (1980). The effects of teacher wait time and questioning quality on middle school science achievement. *Journal of Research in Science Teaching, 17,* 469–475.

Tobin, K. G. (1984, April). *Improving the quality of teacher and student discourse in middle school grades.* Paper presented at the annual meeting of the American Educational Research Association, New Orleans, LA.

Tomlinson, C., & McTighe, J. (2006). *Differentiated instruction and Understanding by Design: Connecting content and kids.* Alexandria, VA: ASCD.

U.S. Department of Health, Education, and Welfare. (1976). *The American Revolution: Selections from secondary school history books of other nations* (HEW Publication No. OE 76-19124). Washington, DC: U.S. Government Printing Office.

Wiggins, G., & McTighe, J. (2005). *Understanding by Design* (Expanded 2nd ed.). Alexandria, VA: ASCD.

Wiggins, G., & McTighe, J. (2007). *Schooling by design.* Alexandria, VA: ASCD.

Wiggins, G., & McTighe, J. (2011). *The Understanding by Design guide to creating high-quality units.* Alexandria, VA: ASCD.

Wiggins, G., & McTighe, J. (2012). *The Understanding by Design guide to advanced concepts in creating and reviewing units.* Alexandria, VA: ASCD.

Wiliam, D. (2007, December–2008, January). Changing classroom practice. *Educational Leadership, 65*(4), 36–42.

Appendix: Annotated Bibliography

Adler, M. J. (1982). *The Paideia proposal: An educational manifesto*. New York: Macmillan.

    Adler describes three different kinds of pedagogy: teaching of content, facilitation of meaning via seminar, and coaching of skills; then he examines the seminar approach in detail.

Ball, W. H., & Brewer, P. (2000). *Socratic seminars in the block*. Larchmont, NY: Eye on Education.

    Ball and Brewer's book extolls the virtues of block scheduling in terms of the extra time that it affords and then explores the use of Socratic seminars within the extended classes of the block.

Bateman, W. L. (1990). *Open to question: The art of teaching and learning by inquiry*. San Francisco: Jossey-Bass.

    Bateman argues that inquiry-based teaching built around effective classroom questioning more effectively evokes curiosity and participation from students than direct instruction.

Copeland, M. (2005). *Socratic circles: Fostering critical and creative thinking in middle and high school*. Portland, ME: Stenhouse.

    Copeland argues that Socratic seminars are capable of improving reading comprehension, class discussion, and critical thinking, and he offers advice and strategies for successfully integrating the Socratic seminar into the classroom environment.

Daniels, H., & Steineke, N. (2004). *Mini-lessons for literature circles*. Portsmouth, NH: Heinemann.

    The fifth chapter of this book focuses on the role of questions in the classroom. The chapter lays out a clear series of definitions—for both educators and students—of what a strong question is, as well as what it is not. Daniels and Steineke argue that the exploration and implementation of discussion and follow-up questions improve student performance.

Dantonio, M., & Beisenherz, P. C. (2001). *Learning to question, questioning to learn: Developing effective teacher questioning practices*. Boston: Allyn and Bacon.

    This study focuses on the "development of productive questioning practices for teachers," offering both theoretical and practical advice for improving questioning within the classroom.

DeZure, D. (1996, September). Asking and answering questions. *Whys and Ways of Teaching, 7*(1), 1–10.

    DeZure's article explores the factors that determine the success of questions (e.g., "the types of questions we ask [according to] Bloom's taxonomy," "the sociocultural dimension to questioning," etc.) and offers advice for assessing and improving questioning methods within the classroom.

Dillon, J. T. (1988). *Questioning and teaching: A manual of practice*. New York: Teachers College Press.

    Dillon's comprehensive analysis draws from all available research at the time in order to consider the role and effect of questioning, on the part of both teacher and student, within the classroom.

Dillon, J. T. (2009). The questions of curriculum. *Journal of Curriculum Studies, 41*(3), 343–359.

    Dillon proposes that the role of questioning is not limited to the relationship between student and teacher within the classroom, but that questioning is also a necessary component to the planning of curricula and the presentation of classroom content. His study explores three orders of questions that must be embedded within effective curricula.

Finkel, D. L. (2000). *Teaching with your mouth shut.* Portsmouth, NH: Boynton/Cook.

This book, specifically the inquiry-based teaching model presented in Chapter 4, discusses the role of both the teacher and questions within the classroom.

Gall, M. (1984, November). Synthesis of research on teachers' questioning. *Educational Leadership, 42*(3), 40–47.

Gall argues that higher-order cognitive questions effect better learning than factual questions. She also suggests that an effective classroom is one in which both teachers and students ask questions.

Hannel, G. I. (2003). *Highly effective questioning: Developing the seven steps of critical thinking.* Phoenix, AZ: Author.

Hannel, aided by a panel of editors, offers a methodology of questioning that allows teachers to shift the purpose of questioning from student assessment to student engagement.

McComas, W. F., & Abraham, L. (2004, October). *Asking more effective questions.* Los Angeles: USC Center for Excellence in Teaching, University of Southern California.

McComas and Abraham create a taxonomy of question types—lower- and higher-order; convergent and divergent—in order to improve the effectiveness of classroom questions. They argue that educators must first ask themselves why they are asking a particular question (i.e., what goals are they hoping to achieve by asking it?) and choose the type of questions based on their goals.

Morgan, N., & Saxton, J. (2006). *Asking better questions* (2nd ed.). Markham, Ontario, Canada: Pembroke.

Morgan and Saxton's book unpacks the topic of questioning by classifying questions and classroom scenarios. They argue that the more complex view of questioning will allow questions to be used appropriately and more effectively.

Raphael, T. E., Highfield, K., & Au, K. H. (2006). *QAR Now: A powerful and practical framework that develops comprehension and higher-level thinking in all students.* New York: Scholastic.

The text explores the relationship between classroom questions and students' reading comprehension abilities, suggesting a positive relationship, as well as practical methods of integrating questioning more effectively into the classroom.

Tienken, C. H., Goldberg, S., & DiRocco, D. (2009, Fall). Questioning the questions. *Kappa Delta Pi Record, 46*(1), 39–43.

This article defines productive questioning, offers a brief history of the literature on questions, and suggests strategies that improve productive questioning in the classroom and its intended corollary, student involvement and participation.

Walsh, J. A., & Sattes, B. D. (2011). *Thinking through quality questioning: Deepening student engagement.* Thousand Oaks, CA: Corwin.

Walsh and Sattes present a framework for questioning and offer many practical strategies to change teaching methods and also track the possible changes that effective questions can bring about in the classroom.

Wilen, W. W. (Ed.). (1987). *Questions, questioning techniques, and effective teaching.* Washington, DC: NEA Professional Library.

This collection compiles nine multiauthored chapters that explore questioning techniques and the relationship between active versus passive learning.

Wilkinson, I. (2009). Questioning. *Education.com.* The Gale Group. Retrieved from http://www.education.com/reference/article/questioning/

Wilkinson provides a brief summary of the current strands of research on questioning. He explores questioning in terms of high and low order; role; and trend—shifting "focus on questions as isolated events to a focus on questions embedded within a larger spatial and temporal context," and shifting from teacher-generated to student-generated questions.

Index

About the Authors

 **Jay McTighe** brings a wealth of experience developed during a rich and varied career in education. He served as director of the Maryland Assessment Consortium, a state collaboration of school districts working together to develop and share formative performance assessments. Prior to this position, Jay was involved with school improvement projects at the Maryland State Department of Education where he directed the development of the Instructional Framework, a multimedia database on teaching. Jay is well known for his work with thinking skills, having coordinated statewide efforts to develop instructional strategies, curriculum models, and assessment procedures for improving the quality of student thinking. In addition to his work at the state level, Jay has experience at the district level in Prince George's County, Maryland, as a classroom teacher, resource specialist, and program coordinator. He also directed a state residential enrichment program for gifted and talented students.

Jay is an accomplished author, having coauthored 10 books, including the best-selling *Understanding by Design* series with Grant Wiggins. He has written more than 30 articles and book chapters, and has published in leading journals, including *Educational Leadership* (ASCD) and *The Developer* (National Staff Development Council).

Jay has an extensive background in professional development and is a regular speaker at national, state, and district conferences and workshops. He has made presentations in 47 states within the United States, in 7 Canadian provinces, and 18 other countries on 5 continents.

Jay received his undergraduate degree from the College of William and Mary, earned his master's degree from the University of Maryland, and completed post-graduate studies at Johns Hopkins University. He was selected to participate in the Educational Policy Fellowship Program through the Institute for Educational Leadership in Washington, DC, and served as a member of the National Assessment Forum, a coalition of education and civil rights organizations advocating reforms in national, state, and local assessment policies and practices. Contact information: Jay McTighe, 6581 River Run, Columbia, MD 21044-6066 USA. E-mail: jmctigh@aol.com.

Grant Wiggins is president of Authentic Education in Hopewell, New Jersey. He earned his EdD from Harvard University and his BA from St. John's College in Annapolis. Grant and his colleagues consult with schools, districts, and state and national education departments on a variety of reform matters. He and his colleagues also organize conferences and workshops, and develop print and web resources on key school reform issues.

Grant is perhaps best known for being coauthor, with Jay McTighe, of *Understanding by Design*, the award-winning and highly successful program and set of materials on curriculum design used all over the world, and of *Schooling by Design*. He is also a coauthor for Pearson Publishing on more than a dozen textbook programs in which UbD is infused. His work has been supported by the Pew Charitable Trusts, the Geraldine R. Dodge Foundation, and the National Science Foundation.

For 25 years, Grant has worked on influential reform initiatives around the world, including Ted Sizer's Coalition of Essential Schools; the International Baccalaureate Program; the Advanced Placement Program; state reform initiatives in New Jersey, New York, and Delaware; and national reforms in China, the Philippines, and Thailand.

Grant is widely known for his work in assessment reform. He is the author of *Educative Assessment* and *Assessing Student Performance*, both published by Jossey-Bass. He was a lead consultant on many state assessment reform initiatives, such as the portfolio project in Vermont and performance assessment consortia in New Jersey and North Carolina.

Several journals have published Grant's articles, including *Educational Leadership* and *Phi Delta Kappan*. His work is grounded in 14 years of secondary school teaching and coaching. Grant taught English and electives in philosophy, coached varsity soccer and cross country, as well as junior varsity baseball and track and field. He also plays in the Hazbins, a rock band. Grant may be contacted at grant@authenticeducation.org.

Related ASCD Resources

At the time of publication, the following ASCD resources were available (ASCD stock numbers appear in parentheses). For up-to-date information about ASCD resources, go to www.ascd.org.

ASCD EDge Group

Exchange ideas and connect with other educators interested in Understanding by Design on the social networking site ASCD EDge® at http://ascdedge.ascd.org/ or log onto ASCD's website at www.ascd.org and click on Research a Topic.

Print Products

Integrating Differentiated Instruction and Understanding by Design: Connecting Content and Kids   Carol Ann Tomlinson and Jay McTighe (#105004)

Making the Most of Understanding by Design   John L. Brown (#103110)

Schooling by Design: An ASCD Action Tool   (#707039)

Schooling by Design: Mission, Action, and Achievement   Grant Wiggins and Jay McTighe (#107018)

Understanding by Design   Expanded 2nd edition   Grant Wiggins and Jay McTighe (#103055)

The Understanding by Design Guide to Creating High-Quality Units   Grant Wiggins and Jay McTighe (#109107)

The Understanding by Design Professional Development Workbook   Jay McTighe and Grant Wiggins (#103056)

DVDs

Connecting Differentiated Instruction, Understanding by Design, and What Works in Schools: An Exploration of Research-Based Strategies with Carol Ann Tomlinson, Jay McTighe, Grant Wiggins, and Robert J. Marzano (#609012)

The Whole Child Initiative helps schools and communities create learning environments that allow students to be healthy, safe, engaged, supported, and challenged. To learn more about other books and resources that relate to the whole child, visit www.wholechildeducation.org.

For more information: send e-mail to member@ascd.org; call 1-800-933-2723 or 703-578-9600, press 2; send a fax to 703-575-5400; or write to Information Services, ASCD, 1703 N. Beauregard St., Alexandria, VA 22311-1714 USA.